Western Hemisphere Department

Commodity Cycles, Inequality, and Poverty in Latin America

Ravi Balakrishnan, Sandra Lizarazo, Marika Santoro, Frederik Toscani, and Mauricio Vargas

INTERNATIONAL MONETARY FUND

Cataloging-in-Publication Data
IMF Library

Names: Balakrishnan, Ravi. | Lizarazo Ruiz, Sandra. | Santoro, Marika. | Toscani, Frederik. | Vargas, Mauricio, 1977- | International Monetary Fund. Western Hemisphere Department, issuing body. | International Monetary Fund, publisher.
Title: Commodity cycles, inequality, and poverty in Latin America / Ravi Balakrishnan, Sandra Lizarazo, Marika Santoro, Frederik Toscani, and Mauricio Vargas.
Other titles: International Monetary Fund. Western Hemisphere Department (Series).
Description: Washington, DC : International Monetary Fund, 2021. | Departmental paper series. | Includes bibliographical references.
Identifiers: ISBN 9781484326091 (paper)
Subjects: LCSH: Prices—Latin America. | Poverty—Latin America. | Equality—Latin America.
Classification: LCC HB235.L25 B35 2021

Ravi Balakrishnan led the staff team and provided overall guidance. Frederik Toscani coordinated analytical inputs and drafting, while Marika Santoro was the lead author of Chapter 4. Frederik Lambert, Lusine Lusinyan, Adrian Peralta Alva, and Marina Mendes Tavares made important contributions to the paper. Adrian Robles, Steve Brito, Catherine Koh, and Cristhian Vera Avellan provided excellent research assistance. Bas Baaker, Pelin Berkmen, Hamid Faruqee, Krishna Srinivasan, Alejandro Werner, and other colleagues in the IMF's Western Hemisphere and other departments provided useful comments and feedback, as did seminar participants in in La Paz, Lima, and Asunción.

Publication orders may be placed online, by fax, or through the mail:
International Monetary Fund, Publication Services
P.O. Box 92780, Washington, DC 20090, U.S.A.
Tel. (202) 623-7430 Fax: (202) 623-7201
E-mail: publications@imf.org
www.imfbookstore.org
www.elibrary.imf.org

Contents

Figures

Executive Summary

Over the past decades, inequality has risen not just in advanced economies but also in many emerging market and developing economies, becoming one of the key global policy challenges. And throughout the 20th century, Latin America was associated with some of the world's highest levels of inequality. Yet something interesting happened in the first decade and a half of the 21st century. Latin America was the only region in the World to have experienced significant declines in inequality in that period. Poverty also fell in Latin America, although this was replicated in other regions, and Latin America started from a relatively low base. Starting around 2014, however, and even before the COVID-19 pandemic hit, poverty and inequality gains had already slowed in Latin America and, in some cases, gone into reverse. And the COVID-19 shock, which is still playing out, is likely to dramatically worsen short-term poverty and inequality dynamics.

Against this background, this departmental paper investigates the link between commodity prices, and poverty and inequality developments in Latin America. To study the impact of the commodity boom of 2000–2014 on the impressive improvements in poverty and inequality the region enjoyed over the same period, it takes a threefold approach: a high-level regional assessment, detailed microdata case studies for Bolivia, Brazil, and Peru, and a heterogenous agent dynamic general equilibrium model calibrated to Bolivia and Paraguay. The paper also discusses the most recent, less-favorable poverty and inequality developments in Latin America in the boom's aftermath and concludes with a discussion of policy options to achieve further social gains in a post-commodity boom World—a task made ever more urgent by the impact of the COVID-19 shock.

During the commodity boom, social gains in Latin America were particularly pronounced in commodity exporters, and much of the progress reflected real labor income gains for lower-skilled workers, especially in services, with a smaller but positive role for government transfers. Spillovers from the commodity sector to the nontradable sectors seem to be at the core of labor income gains for low-skilled labor and are a key driver for the observed poverty and inequality reductions.

Both the case studies and the model simulations show that the impact of a commodity price shock depends on the importance of the sector affected in each country, the type of commodity and its production technology, and government policies. The impact is also stronger on poverty than inequality, not surprisingly, given that the impact on inequality depends on what happens to the full income distribution—gains for everybody reduce poverty but not inequality, for example. Regarding policies, some can have important tradeoffs between the impact on growth and inequality.

The model results show that positive agricultural price shocks appear to have a larger direct effect on poverty and inequality reduction given the relatively high labor intensity (in particular, low-skilled) of the production technology and the low-income level of the majority of the population living in rural relative to urban areas. While reducing poverty, positive energy price shocks have the potential direct effect of increasing income inequality as energy sectors typically employ relatively more skilled labor and the technology is more capital intensive. However, as shown in the case of Bolivia, an increase in energy prices and revenue from royalties seems to lead to a more-than-offsetting indirect effect, including ultimately increasing the demand for auxiliary and other nontradable sectors. Indeed, demand pressures on the nontradable sector appear to be an important indirect effect causing an increase in wages and incomes.

Looking at local data in the country case studies also suggests mineral mining tends to have larger spillover effects than hydrocarbons production because of its higher labor intensity. This shows up in larger shifts in the employment composition and greater poverty reduction in mineral versus hydrocarbons producing municipalities.

An important concern is that local fiscal windfalls associated with the extractive sector might not always have had fully satisfying results. For example, they often led to large increases in public sector employment in oil and gas municipalities, which then contributed to fiscal distress in some cases when the windfall dried up with the end of the boom. In other municipalities with particularly large windfalls on the other hand, issues with absorptive capacity are apparent with unused funds accumulating that could be used productively elsewhere. Given this, when the opportunity exists for substantive reforms to decentralization frameworks, those reforms should aim to minimize horizontal inequities, avoid boom-bust revenue cycles at the local level, and, crucially, clarify the goals of the revenue-sharing agreement. Following the end of the boom, commodity prices remained low for several years. The speed of social gains in Latin America had slowed and, in some cases, partially reversed even before the COVID-19 shock hit. And the COVID-19 shock is unquestionably leading to a further sizable reversal in these gains. Going forward, the region—and especially South American commodity exporters—thus face the critical challenges of first confronting the COVID-19 shock and then achieving further reductions in poverty and inequality. Even before the COVID-19 shock, these challenges remained acute, especially in the case of inequality which remains among the highest in the world. On a subjective level, an average of about 80 percent of Latin Americans described the income distribution in their country as either unfair or very unfair in a 2018 survey, up from about 70 percent in 2013 (and relative to 85 percent in 2001). The immediate task is to dampen the negative impact of the COVID-19 shock on the poor and vulnerable, and transition from emergency crisis support to less costly, post-crisis support. But returning to the structural reform agenda to tackle some of the longstanding factors contributing to high inequality also remains as important as ever.

While there is no silver bullet, policymakers in the region could consider several avenues for reform. Increasing personal income tax revenues by scaling back tax exemptions, avoiding preferential treatments and combating tax evasion while rebalancing spending could help maintain key social transfers and infrastructure spending. Better targeting of social transfers also has an important role to play. Many pension systems in the region have regressive components that should be reformed to reduce inequities while at the same time protecting fiscal sustainability. Ultimately, structural policies, including labor market reform, a renewed focus on education quality and the development of non-resource sectors, possibly through well-calibrated support of the state, are crucial to make an economy resilient to large commodity price swings. Overall, a well-designed and sequenced package of reforms can certainly help limit the fallout from the COVID-19 pandemic and further deepen the social progress made since the turn of the century.

Introduction

Throughout the 20th century, Latin America has been associated with some of the world's highest levels of inequality. Many analysts argue that this is a legacy of colonization and the institutions put in place by the conquistadores (Engerman and Sokoloff 1997, 2000, 2002; Acemoglu, Johnson, and Robinson 2001, 2002). Such a legacy has been linked to: (1) the existence of strong elites, (2) capital market imperfections, (3) inequality of opportunities (in particular, in terms of access to high-quality education), (4) labor market segmentation (for example due to informality), and (5) discrimination against women and non-whites (see Cornia 2014, for a survey).

Latin America has also always been rich in commodities, which attracted the conquistadores in the first place. The commodities ranged from silver in Bolivia to oil in Venezuela, copper in Chile and Peru, and coffee in Brazil and Colombia. The commodity endowments are thought by some to have perpetuated the high levels of inequality. For example, it is argued that commodity-intensive development reduces the returns to education, hampering the impact of expanding education on inequality.[1]

Yet something interesting happened in the first decade and a half of the 21st century. Latin America was the *only* region in the World to have experienced significant declines in inequality in that period (Figure 1). Indeed, inequality has risen not just in advanced economies but in many emerging market and developing economies, becoming the number 1 policy challenge in many of them. Poverty also fell significantly in Latin America, although this was replicated in other regions, and LAC started from a relatively low base (Figure 2).

As noted above, Latin America is a region rich in commodities and from the mid-2000s until 2014 there was a commodity super cycle. Could the decline in inequality and the commodity boom be related? Analyzing this question in the context of Latin America provides the motivation for this departmen-

Figure 1. Gini Coefficient
(Gini coefficient; population weighted average)

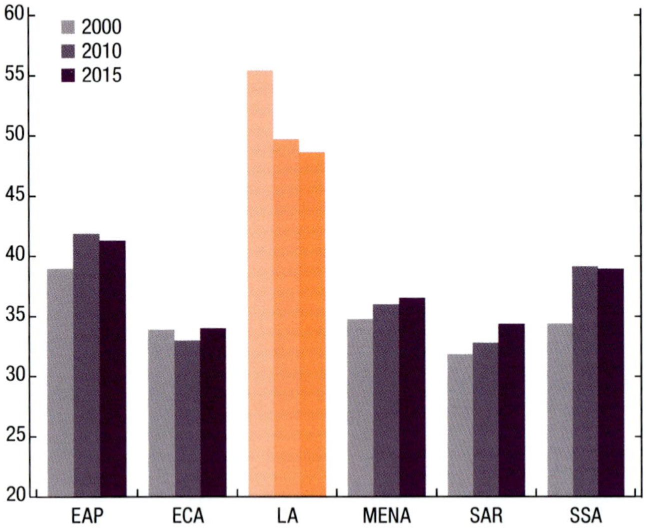

Sources: World Bank, PovcalNet database; and World Bank, World Development Indicators (WDI) database.
Note: For 2015, Latin America (LA) is the average of available values from WDI. Countries include Bolivia, Brazil, Chile, Colombia, Costa Rica, Dominican Republic, Ecuador, El Salvador, Honduras, Panama, Paraguay, Peru, and Uruguay.
EAP = East Asia Pacific; ECA = Europe and Central Asia; LA = Latin America; MENA = Middle East and North Africa; SAR = South Asia; SSA = sub-Saharan Africa.

Figure 2. Poverty Rate
(Percent; headcount ratio at $3.20 a day; 2011 PPP)

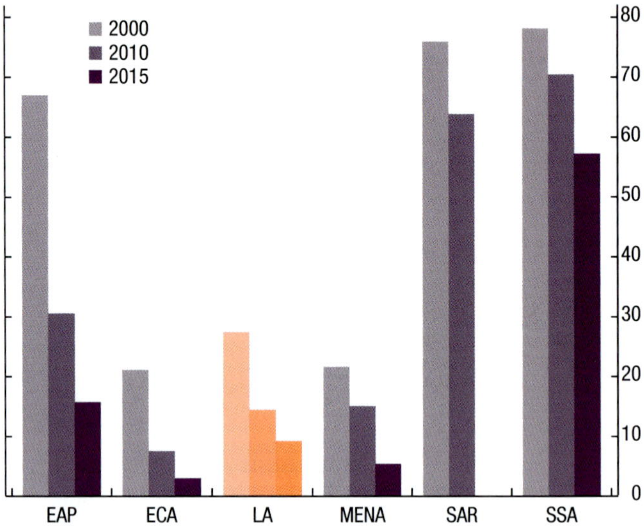

Source: World Bank, World Development Indicators (WDI) database.
Note: For 2015, Latin America (LA) is the average of available values from WDI. Countries include Bolivia, Brazil, Chile, Colombia, Costa Rica, Dominican Republic, Ecuador, El Salvador, Honduras, Panama, Paraguay, Peru, and Uruguay. No data available for SAR in 2015. EAP = East Asia Pacific; ECA = Europe and Central Asia; LA = Latin America; MENA = Middle East and North Africa; PPP = purchasing power parity; SAR = South Asia; SSA = sub-Saharan Africa.

tal paper. The aim is not to explain what drives inequality, which is a vast topic, but to explore the channels via which a commodity boom can impact inequality and other social indicators.

Any study of poverty and inequality, especially when conducted on a cross-country basis, faces several data constraints which warrant a word of caution upfront. Our treatment of poverty and inequality throughout the paper will rely on consumption or income-based measures from household survey data for the simple reason that this is the most widely available data across countries and time. But it is important to stress that there are measurement difficulties associated with this approach and additional dimensions of inequality and poverty that we do not capture.

Wealth inequality is one important dimension of inequality that is not covered in this paper. Recent work suggests that wealth inequality in Latin America is even more pronounced than income inequality (ECLAC 2019), but we are not able to comment on how this might have changed with the commodity boom.

In terms of measurement difficulties, the underrepresentation of very high-income households in household surveys has been much discussed. This also applies to the data used in this study.[2] Cross-country comparability of household survey data can be an additional challenge. The data we use for Latin America are generally harmonized across countries (our main data sources for Latin America are the World Bank's SEDLAC data and the Inter-American Development Bank's Labor Markets and Social Security Information System – SIMS). But when we compare Latin America to other regions comparability is not fully guaranteed given that data for Latin America is generally income-based while for many countries outside Latin America it is consumption based.

In addition, for several parts of this paper we rely on two of the most common ways of aggregating income data into summary statistics on inequality and poverty—the Gini coefficient for inequality and a monetary poverty rate defined relative to either a domestic or an international poverty line for poverty. Of course, there are many other ways to use individual level income data to measure poverty and especially inequality. When possible, we discuss additional measures or present a richer set of indicators focusing on a broader description of the income distribution rather than only one summary statistic.

Finally, a conceptual point is related to our focus on observed inequality of outcomes. An important strand in political philosophy and economics instead argues for a focus on inequality of opportunities. The argument is based on the premise that not all forms of inequality are undesirable. Those related to what one might call "effort" are acceptable or even desirable, while others—those due to circumstances outside an individual's control—are inequitable (Ferreira and Peragine 2016). Societies should thus strive to equalize opportunities while maintaining a principle of reward for effort. Such a focus on equality of opportunities is conceptually appealing but in practice measurement difficulties, especially when trying to look at trends over time, loom large. Given that existing evidence finds a high correlation between inequality of opportunities and observed inequality (Romer and Trannoy 2015), we focus on the latter throughout the paper. Nevertheless, Box 1 discusses some of the available evidence on equality of opportunity in Latin America.

With these caveats in mind, we document in this paper that the period between the turn of the century and around 2014 was one of significant social gains in Latin America, especially in commodity exporters. Much of the progress reflected real labor income gains for lower-skilled workers,

[2]Tax data have been increasingly used to complement household survey data as an important source of income data. Available evidence suggests that the top 1 percent hold as much as 20 (Colombia, Chile, Mexico) to 25 percent (Brazil) of income (ECLAC 2019).

especially in services, with a smaller but important and positive role for government transfers. Spillovers from the commodity sector to the nontradable sectors seem to be at the core of labor income gains for low-skilled labor and are a key driver for the observed poverty and inequality reductions. Since the end of the commodity boom, poverty and inequality have stopped declining and, in a few cases, reversed part of the previous gains. The COVID-19 shock—which has already led to dramatic job losses across Latin America—is likely to substantially worsen short-term poverty and inequality dynamics, making reforms, from fiscal policy to the development of non-resource sectors, even more urgent.

Organization of the Paper

The core of the paper consists of case studies of poverty and inequality developments in select Latin American countries during the commodity boom, both from an empirical (Chapter 3) and a model-based (Chapter 4) perspective. The case studies are framed by a more high-level, descriptive view of cross-country developments since the turn of the century and a discussion of policy priorities.

The paper was written with one coherent narrative in mind, but with room for each chapter to be read individually. In addition, the end of Chapters 3 and 4 have short summaries of the main takeaways of the empirical and model-based case studies, respectively, for readers interested in a more concise overview. Boxes throughout the paper present issues that while not central to the overall narrative, either complement it or offer promising avenues for future work.

The paper proceeds as follows. Chapter 1 sets the stage by first documenting recent trends in inequality and poverty in Latin America. Chapter 2 establishes an empirical link between poverty, inequality, and commodity prices. Chapter 3 then uses micro data for Bolivia, Brazil, and Peru to decompose changes in poverty and inequality and to study the impact of different types of natural resource booms (metals, on shore oil and gas, and offshore oil and gas) on social indicators at the provincial/municipal level. This allows us to disentangle different possible channels—notably a fiscal channel from a direct real economy channel. Chapter 4 complements Chapter 3 by further studying the channels by which commodity cycles affect the distribution of income through the lens of a dynamic general equilibrium model with heterogenous agents. This model is applied to the cases of Bolivia and Paraguay, which again allows a comparison between economies with different types of commodity production. Chapter 5 briefly discusses policy choices during the post-boom years while chapter 6 concludes by drawing out policies which could support Latin America in making further social gains in a world with permanently lower commodity prices.

It would have been desirable to have detailed case studies also for the post-boom period, but at this point it is simply too early to be able to do a comprehensive assessment, due to both the short time period and large lags in data availability of key distributional indicators. This is particularly true with regard to the impact of the COVID-19 shock, given it is still playing out and hit while most of this paper had already been written. Nevertheless, the paper comments on how the COVID-19 shock is impacting the region where possible. In particular, a short discussion of cyclical policy priorities to help mitigate the unprecedented near-term impact of the shock on the poor and vulnerable is included in Chapter 6, before turning to a more detailed look at the structural policies needed to durably further reduce poverty and inequality in Latin America.

Box 1. Measuring (In)equality of Opportunity in Latin America

Building on work by Rawls (1971) and others, equality of opportunity has been theoretically defined as a situation in which outcomes for a population depend only on factors for which persons can be considered responsible (Roemer and Trannoy 2015). Going from this principle to a measurable concept is a non-trivial exercise.

In practice, a two-step process is generally applied. First, an actual distribution of some outcome (income, consumption, etc.) is transformed to obtain a counter-factual distribution that only reflects the unfair component of inequality. In the second step, any desired inequality measure can then be applied to the transformed distribution to obtain a measure of inequality of opportunity. It is easy to see that the practical difficulties associated with the measurement of inequality of opportunities arise in the first step of the process and several different approaches have been proposed in the literature (see Romer and Trannoy 2015; and Ferreira and Peragine for authoritative literature reviews).

Here we focus on the so-called between-types inequality approach. First, individuals are partitioned into types, wherein each type has the same circumstances (such as parental education, race, etc.). Then the actual outcome for each individual is replaced by the mean outcome for his or her type. In other words, the impact of effort is removed by giving everybody with the same exogenous circumstances the same outcome. Given that not all circumstances are observable (and the type-partition is thus imperfect) measuring inequality of opportunity on the resulting distribution will give a lower bound for the actual value (Ferreira and Gignoux 2011).

Somewhat comparable measures of inequality of opportunity as defined above exist for about 40 countries, among them six in Latin American (it is important to stress the limitations of cross-country comparability, not least because the underlying data come from different points in time, often more than a decade apart). In general, Latin American countries are found to have among the highest levels of inequality of opportunity, even among countries of a similar level of development. The lower bound for the share of actual inequality explained by circumstances is found to be about one-third in Guatemala and Brazil, the countries with the highest shares. The studies also yield a number of striking cross-country comparisons in terms of the absolute level: inequality of opportunity in Brazil is found to be more than twice actual inequality in Denmark.

The World Bank has been studying inequality of opportunity in Latin America for many years, using a somewhat different methodology as explained in Barros and others (2009). They look at the question from the perspective of access to basic goods such as sanitation, education, and water. Given the focus on children, it is reasonable to assume that all inequality is due to circumstance rather than effort. The resulting

Box 1. Measuring (In)equality of Opportunity in Latin America *(continued)*

Human Opportunity Index (HOI) correlates highly with general measures of development (if coverage for sanitation is close to 100 percent as it tends to be in richer countries then there can also be no inequality in access to sanitation). Averaging across the education, sanitation, and water components shows progress across Latin American between 2000 and 2014 (latest available year). Southern cone countries (Argentina, Chile, and Uruguay) have the lowest inequality of opportunity according to this measure while countries in Central America (El Salvador, Guatemala, and Honduras) lag substantially behind.

CHAPTER

1 Inequality and Poverty Developments in Latin America Since the Turn of the Century

Panoramic View of Social Gains during the Boom

Poverty and inequality reduction was strong across Latin America during the commodity boom period,[1] especially in South America (Figures 3 and 4).[2] Inequality—as measured by the Gini coefficient—declined in both Central and South America, but significantly more in the latter. In South America, the difference between the 1990s (when poverty and inequality increased) and the boom period is particularly stark.

A large portion of the literature has shown that the widespread decline in inequality across the region during the 2000s was due to a reduction in hourly labor income inequality, and more robust and progressive government transfers (Azevedo, Saavedra, and Winkler 2012; Cornia 2014; Cornia and Martorano 2013; de la Torre, Messina, and Pienknagura 2012; de la Torre and others 2015; Gasparini and Lustig 2011; López-Calva and Lustig 2010;

Part of the material in this chapter, as well as elements from Chapters 2, 3, and 6 formed the core of Chapter 5 of the April 2018 IMF *Regional Economic Outlook: Western Hemisphere Departments*.

[1]The commodity boom for Latin America started during the first decade of the 2000s. While the peak in commodity terms of trade varies across countries, for comparability purposes we define the end of the boom as the start of the 2014 oil price shock.

[2]Given data availability, country coverage includes Argentina, Belize, Bolivia, Brazil, Chile, Colombia, Costa Rica, the Dominican Republic, Ecuador, El Salvador, Guatemala, Honduras, Mexico, Nicaragua, Panama, Paraguay, Peru, and Uruguay. Commodity exporters are determined according to whether net commodity exports surpass 10 percent of total exports plus imports at the time of the October 2015 *World Economic Outlook*, to which Brazil is added given it has the largest estimated natural resource reserves in the region. Hence, the full list of commodity exporters (with main commodity exports in brackets) is: Argentina (soybean meal, corn, soybean oil), Brazil (soybeans, iron ore, crude petroleum), Bolivia (petroleum gas, zinc ore, gold), Chile (copper ore, refined copper, fish), Colombia (crude petroleum, coal briquettes, gold), Ecuador (crude petroleum, bananas, crustaceans), Honduras (coffee, palm oil, bananas), Paraguay (soybeans, soybean meal, bovine meat), and Peru (copper ore, gold, refined petroleum).

Figure 3. Change in Poverty Headcount Ratio
(Percentage points; headcount ratio at $3.1 a day)

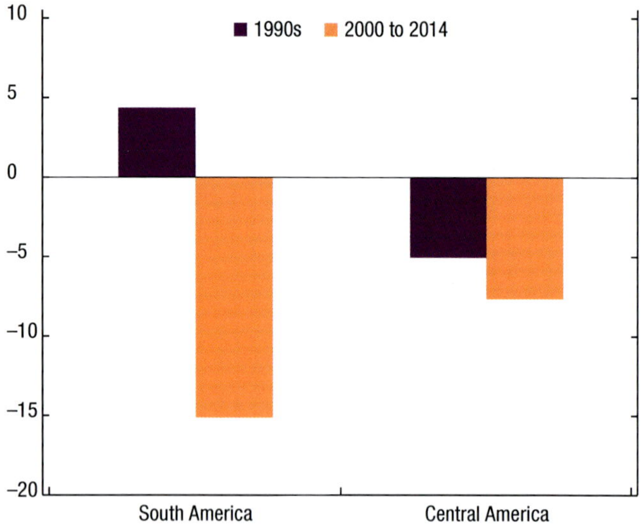

Source: Inter-American Development Bank, SIMS database.
Note: South America is comprised of Argentina, Bolivia, Brazil, Chile, Colombia, Ecuador, Paraguay, Peru, and Uruguay. Central America is comprised of Belize, Costa Rica, El Salvador, Guatemala, Honduras, Mexico, Nicaragua, and Panama.

Figure 4. Change in Average Gini Coefficient
(Gini units)

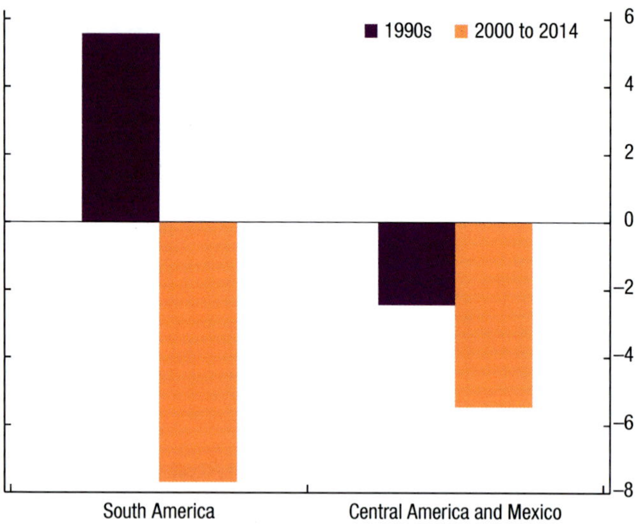

Sources: World Bank, World Development Indicators database; and IMF staff calculations.
Note: South America is comprised of Argentina, Bolivia, Brazil, Chile, Colombia, Ecuador, Paraguay, Peru, and Uruguay. Central America comprises Belize, Costa Rica, El Salvador, Guatemala, Honduras, Nicaragua, and Panama.

Lustig Lopez-Calva, and Ortiz-Juarez 2013).[3] Messina and Silva (2018) provide a detailed discussion of the drivers of changes in wage inequality in Latin America while ECLAC (2017, 2018) document trends in poverty and inequality.

For poverty reduction, and to some degree inequality, an obvious hypothesis is that higher growth across Latin America during the boom period might have been the key driver. Relative to the 1990s, Figure 5 shows that, during the commodity boom period, growth did indeed increase in South America (where poverty fell the most), while in Central America growth was lower although remaining high. Figure 6 shows that the association between GDP

[3]Azevedo, Saavedra, and Winkler (2012) show that, on average, 45 percent of the reduction in the Gini coefficient can be attributed to changes in hourly labor income, which has ranged from 22 percent in Panama to 66 percent in Ecuador. Available evidence suggests that it is the skill premium, or the returns to education, that drives the decline in hourly labor income inequality (Barros and others 2010, 2012; Campos-Vazquez, Esquivel, and Lustig 2012; de la Torre, Messina, and Pienknagura 2012; Cruces and Gasparini 2011). In terms of the contributions of non-labor income, changes in government transfers contributed, on average, 14 percent of the observed regional decline in inequality, while changes in pensions contributed 7 percent. The contribution of changes in returns to capital in Argentina, Brazil, and Mexico is estimated to be small and mostly leading to increased inequality (Lustig, Lopez-Calva, and Ortiz-Juarez 2013). However, household surveys under-estimate income from capital so the effect may have been larger than current estimates indicate. See also Tsounta and Osueke (2014) for a paper exploring the drivers of lower inequality in Latin America.

Figure 5. Average Real GDP Growth
(Percent)

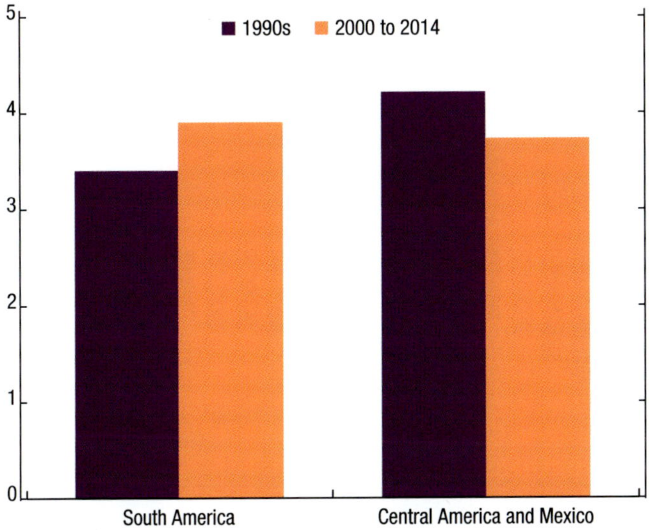

Sources: IMF, World Economic Outlook database; and IMF staff calculations.
Note: South America is comprised of Argentina, Bolivia, Brazil, Chile, Colombia, Ecuador, Paraguay, Peru, and Uruguay. Central America is comprised of Belize, Costa Rica, El Salvador, Guatemala, Honduras, Nicaragua, and Panama.

Figure 6. Average GDP Growth and Change in Poverty Headcount Ratio, 2000–14
(Headcount ratio at $3.10 a day; PPP)

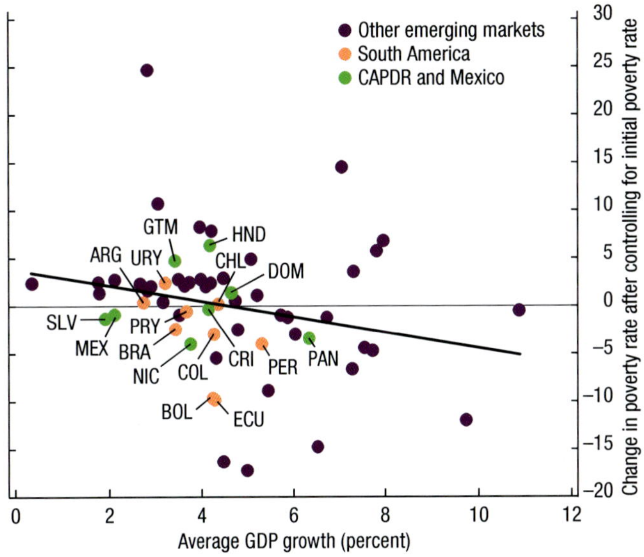

Sources: IMF, World Economic Outlook database; Inter-American Development Bank, SIMS database; and IMF staff calculations.
Note: South America is comprised of Argentina, Bolivia, Brazil, Chile, Colombia, Ecuador, Paraguay, Peru, and Uruguay. Central America is comprised of Belize, Costa Rica, El Salvador, Guatemala, Honduras, Nicaragua, and Panama.
PPP = purchasing power parity. The graph controls for convergence effects. Specifically, the variable on the *y* axis is the residual of a regression of the change in poverty on the initial poverty rate.

growth and poverty reduction for individual countries across emerging regions during the boom period was positive.[4] South American countries are generally below the fitted line, meaning that for every additional percentage point of growth, they reduced poverty by more than other countries. This suggests that factors beyond high growth have been behind the remarkable poverty reduction in South America in the 2000s.[5]

A key question then is why the social gains were greater in South America during the boom relative to other regions. Figure 7 provides a potential link: South America is home to many commodity exporters which experienced a significant boost in their terms of trade relative to other countries. Figures 8 and 9 zoom into the differences in inequality and poverty reduction between

[4]To control for the initial level of poverty, the variable on the *y* axis is the residual of the regression of the change in poverty on the initial poverty ratio.
[5]See Lustig, Lopez-Calva, and Ortiz-Juarez (2013) for another way of looking at this issue. They use a Datt-Ravalion decomposition to decompose the poverty reduction into a "growth" and "redistribution" components.

Figure 7. Average Commodity Terms of Trade Growth during Boom, 2000–14
(Percent)

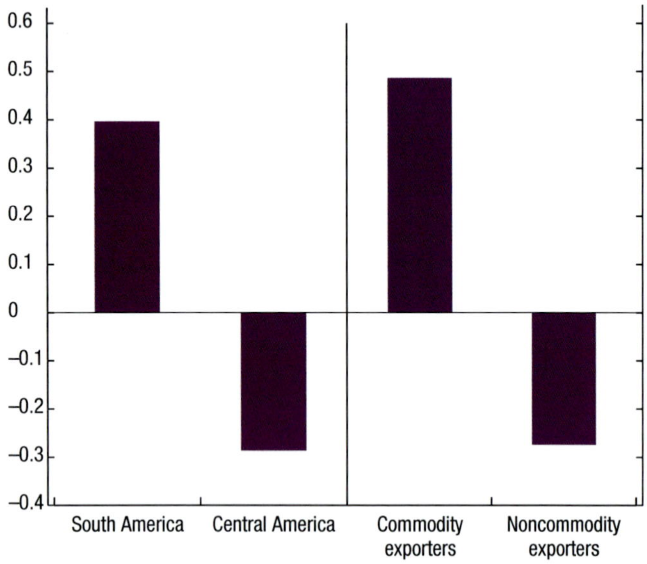

Source: IMF staff calculations.
Note: Terms of trade is the commodity net export price index weighted by GDP (see Gruss 2014). All countries in South America are commodity exporters except Uruguay. All Central American countries are non-commodity exporters except Honduras.

Figure 8. Change in Gini
(Gini units)

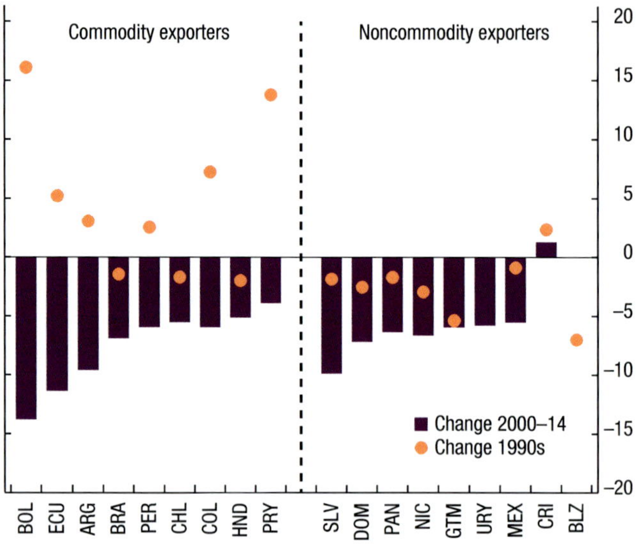

Sources: Inter-American Development Bank, SIMS database; World Bank, World Development Indicators database, and IMF staff calculations.
Note: Brazil, Honduras, Micaragua, and Paraguay use 2001 values for 2000 given data availability. Chile uses 2013 for 2014 data. Country list uses International Organization for Standardization (ISO) country codes.

Figure 9. Change in Poverty Rate
(Percentage points; headcount ratio at $3.10 a day)

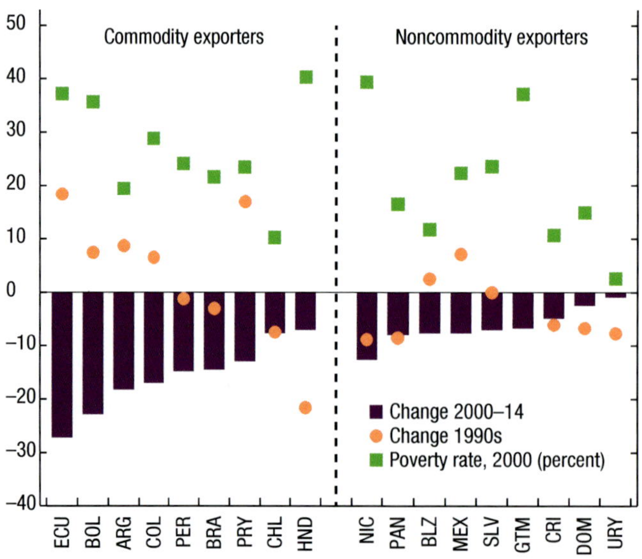

Source: Inter-American Development Bank; and SIMS database.
Note: Colombia uses 2002, and Belize, Brazil, Honduras, and Nicaragua use 2001 values for 2000, given data availability. Argentina uses 2002, after the sharp increase in poverty in 2000–02. Belize uses 2007 (last available data point in SIMS database) instead of 2014, while Chile uses 2013 for 2014. Country list uses International Organization for Standardization (ISO) country codes.

individual commodity exporters and importers. The largest gains on both fronts were made in two countries highly dependent on commodity exports, Bolivia and Ecuador. Indeed, commodity exporters made larger gains in poverty reduction across the board except for Chile and Honduras, which experienced smaller gains than some non-commodity exporters such as Nicaragua and Panama.[6]

For inequality, the same pattern holds but the picture is more mixed, with El Salvador and the Dominican Republic seeing bigger reductions in inequality than several commodity exporters (Chile, Colombia, Paraguay, and Honduras).[7]

This underscores the fact that many factors drive social progress, of which commodity cycles is only one. Indeed, Messina and Silva (2018) argue that supply factors, such as an increasing supply of skilled workers, were likely the key drivers of lower inequality in Central America and Mexico. Lustig (2012) also points to the expansion of cash transfers in Mexico, while IMF (2017) highlights the role of government policies to boost low wages in Uruguay.

Poverty and Inequality Developments from 2014 to 2019[8]

Commodity terms of trade for Latin American commodity exporters peaked in April 2011 when metal prices started to decline.[9] In June 2014 commodity terms of trade then declined sharply as a result of the oil price shock

[6]That poverty fell less in Chile than in other commodity exporters largely reflects the fact that Chile had relatively low poverty rates before the boom: poverty in 2000 stood at 10.3 percent and fell to 2.6 percent by 2013.

[7]The mean poverty reduction during the boom period was statistically significantly larger in commodity exporters than nonexporters. For inequality, the mean reduction is also larger, but the result is not statistically significant.

[8]Comparable cross-country data on poverty and inequality were available until the end of 2018 for most countries at the time of writing and until end-2019 for some.

[9]As a measure of commodity terms of trade, we use an index built by Gruss (2014) and updated in Gruss and Kebhaj (2019). This captures the income gain or loss a country experienced during the period due to commodity price movements. This combines international prices and country-level data on export volumes for each individual commodity. In addition, an increase in the price of imported commodities (for example oil or primary intermediate inputs) is likely to reduce profit margins for firms and disposable income for households. To capture the net income effects from changes in commodity prices, the weights in the price index are based on net exports of each commodity so that commodity price increase would imply a positive (negative) income shock if the country is a net exporter (net importer) of that commodity. A special caveat applies with respect to natural gas exporters (Bolivia in the case of Latin America). Given that there is no worldwide reference price for natural gas, the commodity terms of trade database takes the average of three international hubs. In some instances, this is a poor proxy for the actual price obtained for natural gas exports. In the case of Bolivia, the gas export contracts link prices to crude oil prices. For all countries except Bolivia we use the latest vintage of the Gruss and Kebhaj database. But for Bolivia—when it is shown—we use an earlier vintage which shows higher co-movement with Bolivia's actual export prices.

Figure 10. Commodity Terms of Trade
(Average yearly growth rate; percentage points of GDP)

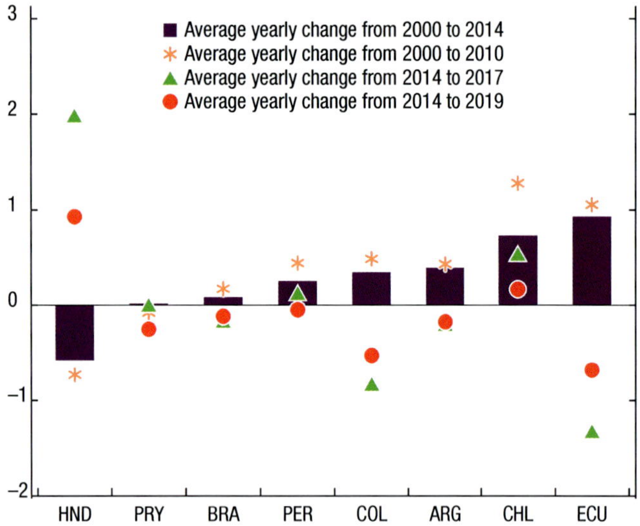

Sources: Gruss and Kebhaj (2019); and IMF staff calculations.
Note: Country list uses International Organization for Standardization (ISO) country codes.

Figure 11. Global Commodity Prices
(Index: 2010 = 100)

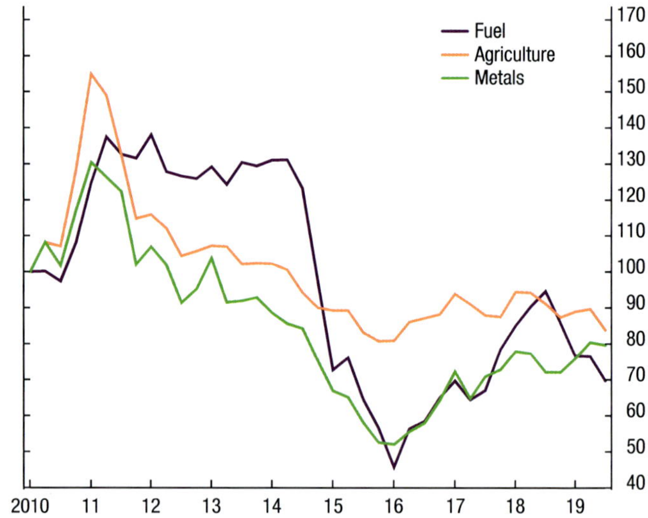

Sources: Bloomberg Finance L.P.; and IMF staff calculations.

(Figures 10 and 11). The biggest reversals came in large oil and natural gas exporters (Bolivia, Colombia, Ecuador). As Figure 10 shows, in Ecuador for example, after increasing by about 1 percent of GDP per year between 2000 and 2014, commodity terms of trade fell strongly after 2014.[10]

For the major metal exporters, Chile and Peru, commodity terms of trade were broadly unchanged between 2014 and 2019—after falling over 2011–14. Metals prices in fact recovered over much of the post-2014 period.

In non-commodity exporters, not much difference in poverty and inequality developments between the boom and post-boom is visible, with most social indicators behaving similarly in both periods. Both poverty and inequality continued to improve over 2014–18/19 (Figures 12 to 16).[11]

But in commodity exporters, poverty reduction came to a halt between the end of the commodity boom and the onset of the COVID-19 crisis (ECLAC 2017, 2018; Figure 12). Looking at labor market developments immediately points to a crucial source of this stagnation. Real wages weakened

[10]Note that Bolivia is omitted from Figure 10 due to the issues identified in footnote 9. Large movements in European natural gas prices lead to the impression of a very large negative commodity terms of trade movement in Bolivia between 2017 and 2019.

[11]Data is until 2018 or 2019 depending on last available data point for each country. In general, when a country does not have data for a specific year, we use the closest available year instead.

Figure 12. Annualized Change in Poverty Headcount Ratio
(Percentage points; headcount ratio at $3.1 a day)

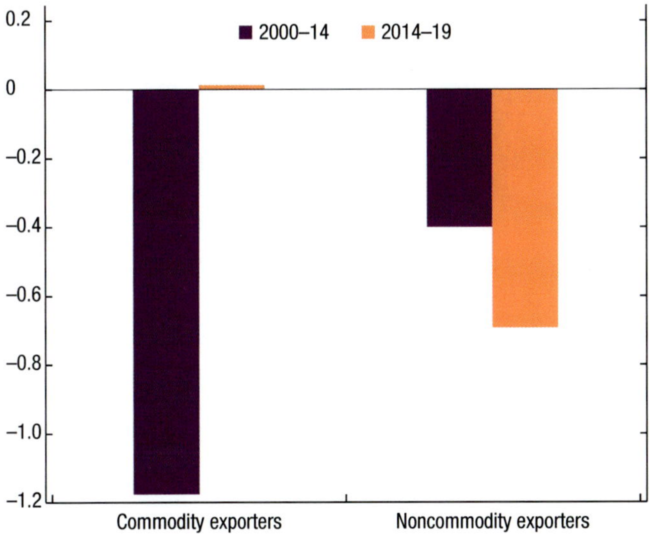

Source: Inter-American Development Bank, SIMS database.

Figure 13. Average Annual Real Monthly Wage Growth in the Primary Occupation
(Percent)

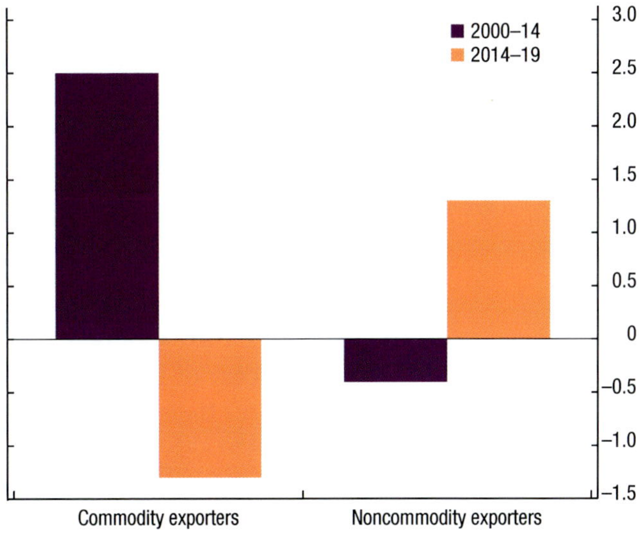

Source: Inter-American Development Bank, SIMS database.

Figure 14. Average Annual Change in the Employment Rate
(Percent)

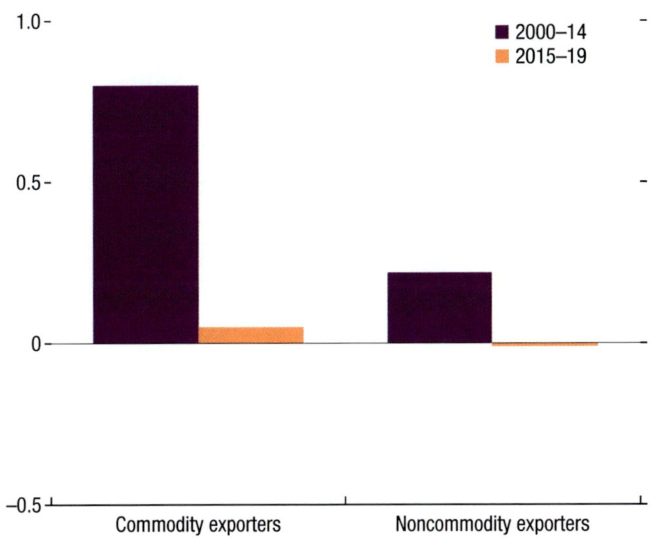

Sources: Inter-American Development Bank; and SIMS database.

Figure 15. Change in Gini Index
(Gini units)

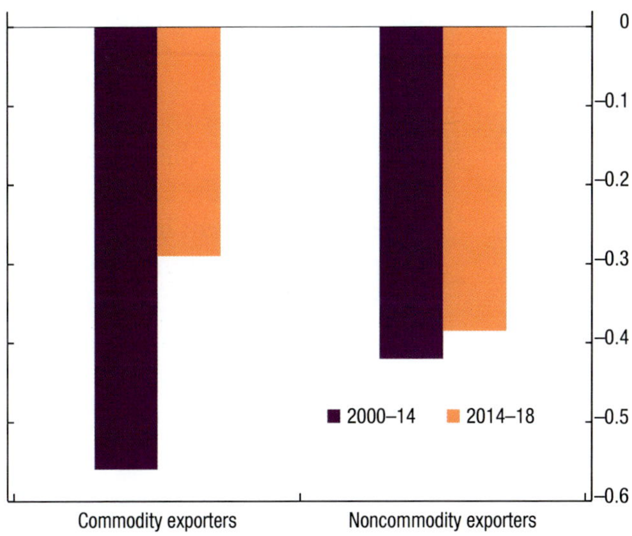

Sources: World Bank, World Development Indicators; and IMF staff estimates.

and employment growth slowed, both in stark contrast to the boom times (Figures 13 and 14). But while poverty increased somewhat in a few cases with economic crises such as Argentina and Brazil, on average the impressive gains of the boom did not so much reverse as stagnate. The impact on inequality has been even less negative, as inequality in fact continued to fall in commodity exporters on average (Figure 15). We will discuss why the link between poverty and commodity prices might be stronger than with inequality in later chapters.

Much starker than the reversal in actual poverty and inequality observed in Latin America after the end of the commodity boom, has been a worsening of perceptions of the fairness of the income distribution. After improving strongly over 2001–13, perceptions worsened over 2013–18, with more than 80 percent of Latin Americans saying that they perceive the income distribution in their country to be unfair or very unfair (Latinbarómetro, see also Box 2).[12]

Early Evidence on the Impact of the COVID-19 Shock on Poverty and Inequality

It is against this backdrop of a new commodity price normal, a stagnation or slowdown in social progress and worsening perceptions of fairness that the COVID-19 shock hit Latin America. The direct effect of the shock has been an unprecedented contraction in economic activity in 2020. This has led to historic jobs losses across the region. Total employment in LA5 (Brazil, Chile, Colombia, Peru and Mexico) fell by 30 percent on average between January and May 2020, the largest four-month contraction on record. Employment losses beyond the largest economies were similar, for example employment fell by 15 percent in Bolivia from February to May and an equivalent contraction was seen in Ecuador from December to May/June. The largest job losses were concentrated among more vulnerable segments of society, most prominently informal workers in the services sector with lower levels of education (IMF, 2020b). An online survey conducted by Bottan, Hoffman and Vera-Cossio (2020) in a large number of LAC countries found that job and income losses were more likely among respondent who had lower income pre-COVID.

Lustig and others (2020) present a comprehensive forward-looking microsimulation exercise on the impact of the crisis on poverty and inequality in Argentina, Brazil, Colombia and Mexico, taking into account also the offset

[12]Latinobarómetro is a Sanitago de Chile based non-governmental organization. Annual surveys on Latin American public opinion are available online at http://www.latinobarometro.org/lat.jsp for the time period 1996–2018. The margin of error per country and year is roughly +/- 3 percent.

offered by expanded social assistance. Their results point to an increase of 4–9 percentage points in the poverty rate in all countries and an increase in the Gini of 0.02–0.04 when the government's policy response is not included. But in Argentina and Brazil the worsening of social outcomes will be strongly mitigated by emergency government assistance while it is in place.[13] As noted by several commentators, there is thus an important risk that the shock will materially worsen poverty and inequality, not just immediately but over the next years.[14] We will come back to the policy challenges this sudden deterioration in social progress entails in Chapter 6.

[13]For Brazil, survey data show that labor income losses were large across the income distribution but the bottom decile was most affected with a decline of around 30 percent. The poverty rate in May would have increased by as much as 8 percentage point based only on labor income. But preliminary evidence suggests that broad-based emergency cash transfers more than offset the labor income losses of the bottom 40 percent of the income distribution, avoiding any increase in poverty and inequality, at least temporarily (IMF 2020b). Underlying data come from IBGE's PNAD-Covid.

[14]https://publications.iadb.org/publications/english/document/Labor-markets-of-Latin-America-and-the-Caribbean-in-The-Face-of-The-Impact-of-COVID-19.pdf; https://observatoriolaboral-bid.herokuapp.com/empleo/; https://www.nytimes.com/2020/07/11/world/americas/coronavirus-latin-america-inequality.html; https://www.scribd.com/document/463531085/Nota-Macroeconomica-Universidad-de-Los-Andes.

Box 2. Inequality Perceptions: "How Fair is the Income Distribution in Your Country?"

An overwhelming majority of respondents across Latin America believe that the income distribution in their country is either unfair or very unfair (Figure 2.1, data from Latinobarometro). Looking at how the average of these survey answers have changed over time reveals an interesting pattern—in 2001, 11 percent of respondents perceived the income distribution to be fair or very fair. This rose to 23 percent at the end of the commodity boom in 2013 and fell back to 16 percent in 2018. The pattern holds across Latin American countries with few exceptions, but the magnitude of the improvement varies strongly, with the largest positive changes in Ecuador, Panama, and Uruguay. On the other hand, during 2013–18 perceptions of the fairness of the income distribution worsened across the region with the largest reversals in Venezuela, Ecuador, and Panama. Despite the worsening during 2013–18, respondents in Bolivia and Ecuador were the most likely to perceive income as fairly distributed in 2018, while respondents in Venezuela and Chile were the least likely (Figure 2.2).

It is not straight-forward to link the change in country-level perceptions to measured changes in the Gini coefficient. Over the boom period, the perceived improvement in fairness correlates well with the objective fall in income inequality (correlation 0.59). But over 2013–18 the correlation is insignificant (and has in fact the wrong sign).

Figure 2.1. Survey—How Fair is the Income Distribution in Your Country?
(Average for all of Latin America)

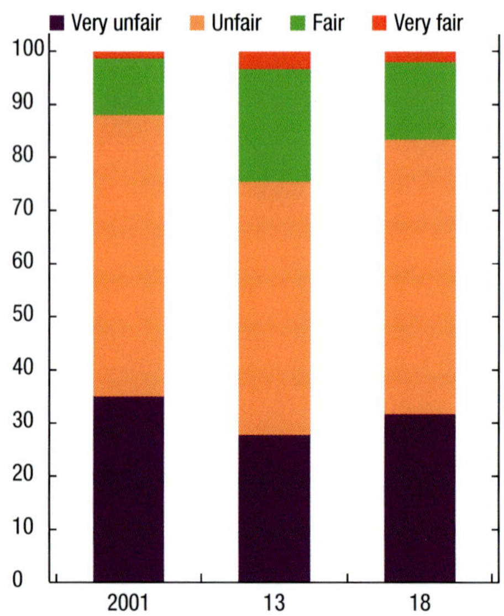

Sources: Latinobarometro; and IMF staff calculations.

Figure 2.2. Survey—How Fair is the Income Distribution in Your Country?
(Change in share of respondents who say Fair or Very Fair between 2001–13 and 2013–18 and share who say fair or very fair in 2018)

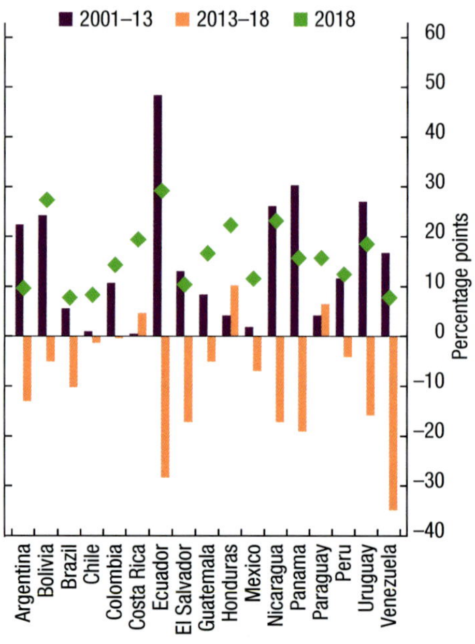

Sources: Latinobarometro; and IMF staff calculations.

CHAPTER

2 The Link Between Commodity Cycles, Poverty, and Inequality

Building on the suggestive evidence in the previous section of a link between commodity price cycles and social outcomes, we test the empirical relationship between commodity cycles and changes in inequality and poverty in this chapter. As in Chapters 3–4, we primarily focus on the boom period in this chapter given the longer time period available for study and return to the post-boom period in Chapter 5.

Is There a Statistical Association?

What is the relationship between social indicators and the commodity cycle? The correlation between the reduction in poverty and inequality during the boom period and the change in commodity terms of trade points to an interesting story (Figure 16). For non-commodity exporters, there is no clear association between changes in commodity terms of trade and those in poverty and inequality. For commodity exporters, however, the relationship is strong, particularly so for poverty. The size of poverty reduction is directly proportional to the growth rate of the commodity terms of trade in commodity exporters.[1] For inequality, the relationship for commodity exporters is not as strong as for poverty but it is still clearly visible. A closer relationship between the commodity cycle and poverty (rather than inequality) seems to be an empirical regularity found throughout this paper.

[1]While Honduras is classified as a commodity exporter given high net commodity exports, its commodity terms of trade declined since it exports non-extractive commodities and imports extractive ones that saw their prices increase by more. Consequently, commodity price changes led to a negative wealth effect for Honduras and poverty fell significantly less than in most other Latin American countries.

Figure 16. Commodity Terms of Trade, Poverty, and Gini Coefficient

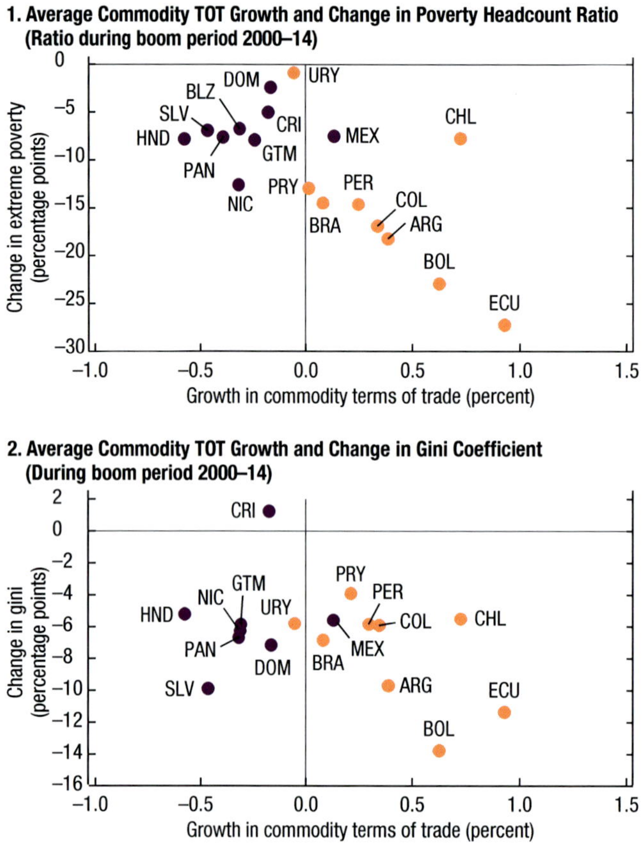

Sources: Inter-American Development Bank, SIMS database; Gruss and Kebhaj (2019) for Bolivia Gruss (2014); World Bank, World Development Indicators database; and IMF staff calculations.
Note: Purple dots correspond to CAPDR and Mexico; Orange dots to South America. CAPDR is comprised of Central America, Panama, and the Dominican Republic. For poverty, Chile uses 2013 values for 2014 due to data availability. Colombia uses 2002, and Belize, Brazil, Honduras, and Nicaragua use 2001 values for 2000, given data availability. Argentina uses 2002, after the sharp increase in poverty in 2000–02. Belize uses 2007 (last available data point in SIMS database) instead of 2014, while Chile uses 2013 for 2014. Country list uses International Organization for Standardization (ISO) country codes.

Panel Regression Analysis

As an alternative way to test for the existence of a relationship between inequality and commodity cycles, we estimate the following panel regression:

$$y_{i,t} = \alpha_i + \beta x_{i,t} + \delta v_{i,t-1} + \epsilon_{i,t}$$

Table 1. Relationship between Commodity Export Prices and Inequality

Panel FE	(1)	(2)	(3)	(4)
	Commodity Exporters		Non-commodity Exporters	
	All	LAC	All	LAC
Variables	(log) Gini (disp. Income)	(log) Gini (disp. Income)	(log) Gini (disp. Income)	(log) Gini (disp. Income)
Commodity Terms of	−0.109	−.311*	0.022	0.552
Trade, weighted by GDP	0.068	0.135	0.135	0.302
Control	GDP per capita (*t* - 1)	GDP per capita (*t* - 1)	GDP per capita (*t* - 1)	GDP per capita (*t* - 1)
Country Fixed Effects	Yes	Yes	Yes	Yes
Number of Countries	53	13	104	16
Observations	1,350	358	2,885	344

Sources: Gruss (2019); Standardized World Income Inequality Database (SWIID); and IMF staff calculations. Data are from 1961 when available.
Note: $*p < 0.10$; $**p < 0.05$; $***p < 0.01$.

where $y_{i,t}$ is the (log) Gini coefficient of country i in year t and $x_{i,t}$ is country i's commodity terms of trade (see Gruss and Kebhaj [2019], which updates Gruss [2014]).[2] β is the coefficient of interest. and α_i is a country fixed-effect Given that we have a long panel for some countries, we also include the lagged level of GDP per capita $v_{i,t-1}$, to control for the impact of the stage of development on inequality. The regressions here are clearly simplistic and are only intended to show correlations which can further motivate the analysis in the remainder of the paper.

We use yearly data on income distribution from several sources. For the largest sample of countries, we use the Standardized World Income Inequality Database (SWIID).[3] For Latin America, we also complement this by using data from the Socio-Economic Database for Latin America and the Caribbean (SEDLAC). This dataset is compiled by the World Bank and CEDLAS, which harmonizes inequality, poverty and other distributional measures (for example, income decile shares) across different household surveys in Latin American countries.[4] We use the full sample available from 1961 until 2018 as far as data are available for the regressions shown in Table 1.

[2]For the Gini index, we use the measure derived from disposable (post-tax and transfers) income (Gini Net) as it already controls for the impact of fiscal policies on households' budgets. The annual weight of each commodity used to construct the commodity terms of trade is given by the share of net exports in output: $\omega_{i,j,\tau} = \frac{x_{i,j,\tau} - m_{i,j,\tau}}{GDP_{i,\tau}}$ where $x_{i,j,\tau}(m_{i,j,\tau})$ denotes the exports (imports) value of commodity j of country i in year τ, expressed in US dollars; and $GDP_{i,\tau}$ denotes country i's nominal GDP is US dollars in year τ (Gruss and Kebhaj, 2019 p. 10). A 1 percentage point change in the commodity terms of trade index can be interpreted as a change in aggregate disposable income equivalent to 1 percentage point of GDP.

[3]See Solt (2016). The SWIID currently incorporates comparable Gini indices of disposable and market income inequality for 192 countries for as many years as possible from 1960 to the present; it also includes information on absolute and relative redistribution.

[4]http://www.cedlas.econo.unlp.edu.ar/wp/en/estadisticas/sedlac/. The data for certain countries are not always fully comparable over time due to changes in the methodology of the underlying household surveys. See https://dataviz.worldbank.org/t/LCSPP/views/23_DataAvailabilitySP2019/DataAvailability?iframeSizedToWindow=true&:embed=y&:showAppBanner=false&:display_count=no&:showVizHome=no.

Table 2. Commodity Terms of Trade and Income Share by Decile in Commodity Exporters

Variables	(1) Decile 1	(2) Decile 2	(3) Decile 3	(4) Decile 4	(5) Decile 5	(6) Decile 6	(7) Decile 7	(8) Decile 8	(9) Decile 9	(10) Decile 10
Commodity Terms of Trade, weighted by GDP	0.037**	0.059**	0.066**	0.07**	0.075**	0.078**	0.081***	0.072***	0.035	−0.57***
	−0.013	−0.02	−0.023	−0.025	−0.027	−0.026	−0.023	−0.017	−0.022	−0.16
Country Fixed Effects	Yes	Yes	Yes	Yes	Yes	Yes	Yes	Yes	Yes	Yes
Control	GDP per capita	GDP per capita	GDP per capita	GDP per capita	GDP per capita	GDP per capita	GDP per capita	GDP per capita	GDP per capita	GDP per capita
Period	2000–14	2000–14	2000–14	2000–14	2000–14	2000–14	2000–14	2000–14	2000–14	2000–14
Observations	114	114	114	114	114	114	114	114	114	114
R-Squared	0.236	0.213	0.205	0.197	0.206	0.217	0.246	0.288	0.094	0.258
Number of Countries	9	9	9	9	9	9	9	9	9	9

Sources: Gruss (2019); Socio-Economic Database for Latin America and Caribbean (CEDLAS and World Bank); and IMF staff calculations.
Note: $*p < 0.10$; $**p < 0.05$; $***p < 0.01$.

Estimates confirm the general view from the scatter plots in the previous section that there exists a negative relationship between a change in the commodity price index and the Gini coefficient in the case of Latin American countries that are commodity exporters. In other words, a positive increase in commodity net export prices is associated with a fall in income inequality. Interestingly, while negative, the relationship is not significant when all commodity exporters are included in the sample and the point estimate is also smaller, suggesting that something special did happen in Latin America.

We now focus on Latin America, with a closer look at which income groups really benefited from the reduction in the Gini coefficient associated with the commodity boom in Latin America. To do so we turn to data on income shares by decile for Latin American commodity exporters taken from SEDLAC. Due to data availability, we cover only the period starting in 2000 here. Mirroring the above specification, Table 2 reports regressions of the share of income by decile on commodity terms of trade as well as GDP per capita and country fixed effects for commodity exporters in Latin America.[5]

The resulting associations are much stronger than the rather weak correlations recovered in Table 1. Table 2 shows that income shares of the first to eighth deciles increased significantly during the boom, while the share of the top decile declined. Since both low- and medium- to high-income segments gained, the poverty result is stronger than the inequality one. Nevertheless, inequality did tend to fall given the share of income going to the highest decile fell substantially on average. Interestingly, and related, the results are quantitatively strongest for upper middle deciles (5–7) especially when compared to the lowest ones. Note that poverty reduction depends on developments close to the poverty line, namely the 2nd–4th decile depending on the country.[6]

[5]We only include commodity exporters in the sample here given that this is the focus of the analysis.
[6]For example, in Bolivia nearly 40 percent of the population were below the poverty line in 2000.

What Are the Channels during the Boom Phase?

The statistical relationship naturally leads to the question of the channels through which the commodity cycle could influence social indicators. Essentially, a commodity boom is a positive wealth shock that propagates through the economy via various channels (including those related to "Dutch disease"):[7,8]

Market/Private-sector Channels

- First, the booming commodity sector expands. This draws in labor and other resources. Higher labor demand pushes up real wages and/or employment. It can also reduce the skills premium, depending on the relative labor intensity of the commodity sector.[9]
- Second, improved terms of trade and the expansion of the commodity sector have spillovers to other sectors. With higher wealth and incomes, domestic demand increases, benefiting the nontradable sector. Higher investment by the commodity sector, leading to more construction for example, is another way through which the positive wealth shock feeds into the economy, again expanding the nontradable sector.
- Third, changes in relative wages (a compression in the skills premium if the commodity sector and the nontradable sector are intensive in unskilled labor) will benefit more skill intensive sectors and lead to further reallocation.[10]

Overall, the above channels should lead to more employment in the commodity and the nontradable sectors. The impact on the non-commodity tradable sector is not clear ex ante. On the one hand, the classic natural resource curse ("Dutch Disease") could be operating—higher demand expands the nontradable sector but crowds out the non-commodity sector due to a more appreciated real exchange rate.[11] On the other hand, if key tradable inputs are provided locally, there can be positive spillovers from the commodity sector to the manufacturing sector, as has been shown for the US.[12] Given

[7]See, for example, Alberola and Benigno (2017).

[8]On the larger question of the long-term impact of natural resource abundance for GDP growth and development, there is no consensus. Van der Ploeg (2011), for example, shows that results supporting "the natural resource curse" are sensitive to sample periods and countries.

[9]Oil and gas production, for example, is substantially less labor intensive than agriculture but is more intensive in skilled labor.

[10]Benguria, Saffie, and Urzua 2018.

[11]Harding and Venables 2016.

[12]Allcott and Keniston (2018) demonstrate positive spillovers of the oil and gas sector to manufacturing in the US. Michaels (2011) finds a similar positive result for the US.

the relatively narrow initial manufacturing base in most Latin American countries, both effects might be modest, but commodity booms are likely to hamper export diversification to some degree.

In terms of social outcomes, the expansion of the commodity and non-tradable sectors, and the related increase in wages, should reduce poverty if those sectors employ workers from the lower end of the income distribution. Additionally, inequality will fall if the expanding sectors are intensive in low-skilled labor, causing the skills premium to decline.

Fiscal Channels

The positive wealth shock is also transmitted via higher fiscal revenues and expenditures:

- Higher government investment operates similarly to higher commodity sector investment. It leads to more domestic demand, for example via increased construction, with a resulting impact on wages and thus poverty and inequality.[13]
- Larger transfers will have a direct impact on poverty and inequality, especially if the transfers are targeted toward lower-income individuals.

Other General Equilibrium Effects

The wealth shock can be transmitted via other general equilibrium effects, for example via the financial system or through second-round effects such as migration to urban areas.

Regional Macroeconomic Evidence

In aggregate, commodity booms should reduce poverty and inequality through labor market developments and fiscal transfers.[14] And indeed, these mechanisms seem to have played out in the region. Public investment and employment growth were higher in commodity exporters than importers (Figures 17 and 18). In line with the results of De la Torre and others (2015), commodity exporters also experienced significantly larger real labor income gains than non-commodity exporters across all skill levels (Figure 19). Low-skilled workers gained the most, compressing the skills premium and reducing inequality in both commodity

[13]Of course, public and private investment can also expand supply not just demand.

[14]Note that the vast majority of households in Latin America outside the highest-income segments do not receive any capital income so that transfer and labor income explain the overwhelming fraction of total income for them.

Figure 17. Public Investment in Latin America
(Percent of GDP)

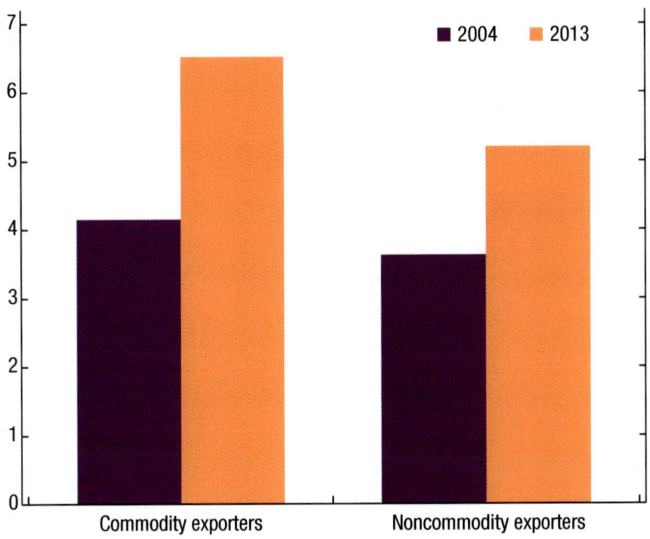

Sources: IMF, World Economic Outlook database; and IMF staff calculations.

Figure 18. Total Employment Growth
(Percent)

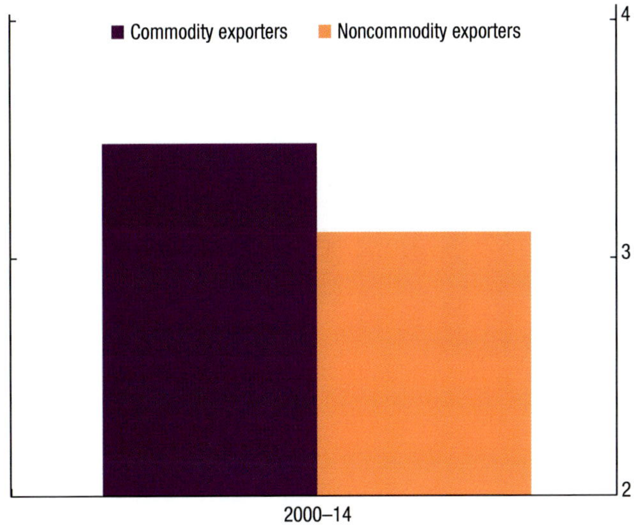

Sources: Inter-American Development Bank; and SIMS database.

Figure 19. Real Labor Income Growth by Educational Level
(Percent)

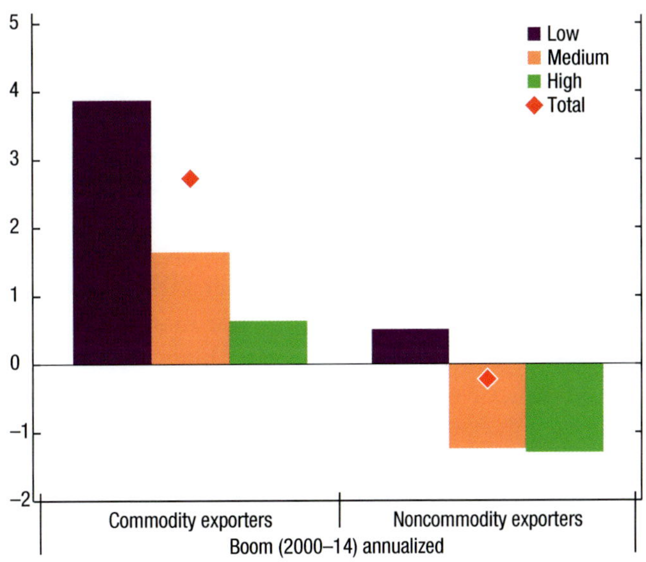

Source: Inter-American Development Bank, SIMS database.

Figure 20. Skill Premium Change in the 2000s
(Percentage point change in the ratio of hourly wage, high to low education)

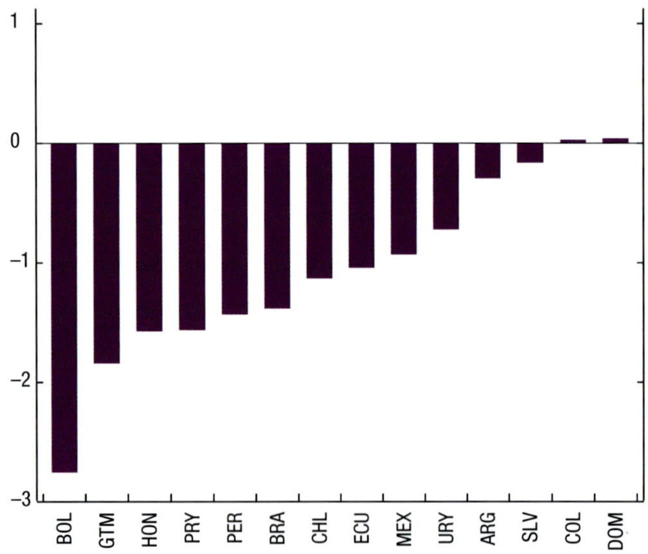

Sources: Socio-Economic Database for Latin America and Caribbean (CEDLAS and World Bank); and IMF staff calculations. Country list uses International Organization for Standardization (ISO) country codes.

Figure 21. Average Government Transfers in Latin America
(Percent of GDP)

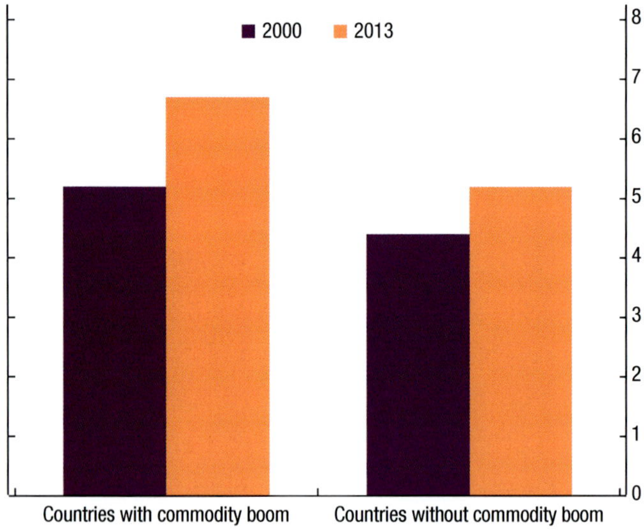

Sources: IMF, World Economic Outlook database; and IMF staff calculations.

exporters and non-exporters (Figure 20) but due to different underlying wage dynamics.[15] In addition to labor income, government transfers also increased more in commodity exporters than non-exporters, further contributing to greater poverty and inequality gains in commodity exporters (Figure 21).

An important backdrop to the analysis is the structure of Latin American labor markets. As laid out in the October 2019 Western Hemisphere Department Regional Economic Outlook, labor markets in the region tend to be characterized by low labor productivity, high informality, and a rigid regulatory environment contributing to strong duality between well-protected formal sector jobs and unprotected informal sector jobs (IMF 2019a). The impact of the commodity boom would likely have been different in a setting without a large pool of workers in relatively low productivity occupations.

[15]See Messina and Silva (2018) for a detailed discussion of demand and supply factors underlying the skill premium compression during the boom. They note that while an increase in high-skilled labor supply was an important factor, the demand factors tied to the commodity boom discussed in this chapter were also key drivers.

Disentangling the Channels

Disentangling the above-discussed channels is a challenging task. As all approaches have their advantages and disadvantages, we tackle the question from several angles to try and provide comprehensive insights. Detailed case studies are conducted for Bolivia, Brazil, Paraguay. and Peru.

In Chapter 3, we first use national level household survey data to decompose changes in the income distribution into changes which are due to fiscal redistribution versus those that stem from changes in labor income. This allows us to comment on whether poverty and inequality gains during the commodity boom were mainly driven by government transfers or the labor market. The exercise also allows us to look at the sectoral composition of labor income changes and we are thus able to comment on which sectors contributed the most to the observed gains. Second, we use local level data to zoom in on the mechanisms. In particular, we exploit regional variations in the amount as well as type of natural resource produced (mineral mining vs onshore oil vs offshore oil) to better understand the direct market effect and fiscal windfall. This takes us one step further than the previous exercise since the decompositions cannot discriminate between labor income gains mediated by the public sector and labor income gains due to pure market effects.

Both exercises in Chapter 3 have their own drawbacks; however, while allowing for a clean identification, local level data do not provide conclusions about the impact at the national level. And while the Shapley decompositions are done at the national level, they do not allow us to discriminate between the channels via which labor income increases.

To complement the analysis of Chapter 3, we thus use simulations from a heterogenous agent DGE model in Chapter 4. The local level analysis in Chapter 3 focuses on the impact of the extractive sector, but in Chapter 4 we define commodities more broadly to include both extractive industries and the agricultural sector. The model allows us to trace out and quantify the channels by which agricultural and energy commodity price shocks affected inequality, poverty, and growth during the 2000s. They also allow us to see the impact of various tax and spending policies.

Chapter

3 Micro Data Case Studies of the Boom: Bolivia, Brazil, and Peru

This chapter presents microdata case studies for Bolivia, Brazil, and Peru, three important commodity exporters in Latin America. It also briefly analyzes dynamics in a commodity importer—Mexico—which provides an interesting contrast to the trends seen in commodity exporters.

Bolivia

Overview of Extractive Sector in Bolivia

Bolivia produces both hydrocarbons (mainly natural gas) as well as minerals. Oil and gas production started early in the 20th century but only with the large gas discoveries of the 1990s did Bolivia become a major hydrocarbon player. The so-called megacampos allowed Bolivia to increase its gas production volume by a factor of 8 between 1999 and 2015 and made large-scale gas exports to Brazil and Argentina possible. Bolivian gas today covers one-third of total Brazilian gas demand. Bolivia is also still an important producer of metals, notably zinc, silver, and gold but metals contributed relatively less to GDP, exports, and fiscal revenues than hydrocarbons during the boom. At the peak in 2014, the sum of hydrocarbon and metal mining accounted for a total of close to 15 percent of GDP, 80 percent of export revenues and 35 percent of fiscal revenues.

Bolivia collects significant fiscal rents from the resource sector, with the "government take" in oil and gas production estimated at more than 70 percent. The effective royalty rate for hydrocarbon production is 50 percent—an 18 percent royalty plus a 32 percent direct tax on hydrocarbons. A large share of royalties goes to subnational units. Out of the total 18 percent hydrocarbon royalty, 11 percent go to producing departments, 6 percent stays with the central government and 1 percent goes to the lightly populated departments of Pando and Beni. The 32 percent hydrocarbon tax (IDH) is allocated in a more complicated way, going to both producing and non-producing departments as well as municipalities.[1] Mining royalties are distributed only to producing departments and municipalities, with an 85–15 split between the two.

Stylized Facts on Inequality, Poverty, and Natural Resource Production in Bolivia

Bolivia, one of the poorest countries in South America, dramatically reduced inequality and poverty over the boom period even when compared to peers in Latin America. Over the boom years, Bolivia's Gini coefficient fell by close to nine basis points (8.7 points). In the mid-90s, Bolivia had a Gini coefficient well above the Latin America average, but it now has a level below several of its peers. Interestingly, and similar to many Latin American peers, Bolivia's net and market Gini do not differ much, indicating that transfers and other redistributive policies might not be a key driver for lower inequality.

Household survey data show that labor income of low-skilled workers increased strongly over the boom period (2001–13).[2] Looking at the change in labor income by decile, we can see that there were gains across most categories except for the very top ones (see Figure 22), a result that closely mirrors the one highlighted in the cross-country regressions for the whole of LAC in Table 2. Furthermore, when we discriminate by education level, we find that income gains were large for low-skilled workers, but actually negative for high-skilled ones (Figure 23).

Figure 24 breaks down changes in real per capita labor income and employment by productive sector rather than by education or income level. In terms of employment growth, the biggest winners were the extractive sector and commerce, in line with the previous discussion on channels. In terms of numbers of jobs created, the broad services sector contributed the most, in part reflecting its size. Overall, employment growth came from extractive and nontradable sectors. Interestingly, the picture is more mixed for real wage growth. Average wages in the extractive sector fell, likely reflecting a compositional effect, with the number of informal (poorly paid) miners increasing faster than employees in larger, capital-intensive mines during the boom.

[1]Simplifying somewhat, producing departments receive 1 percent, producing municipalities 3 percent, non-producer departments 8 percent and the remaining 20 percent stay with the central government.

[2]See Vargas and Garriga (2015).

Figure 22. Income Distribution in Bolivia
(Real Bs. for 2001, 2006 and 2013)[1]

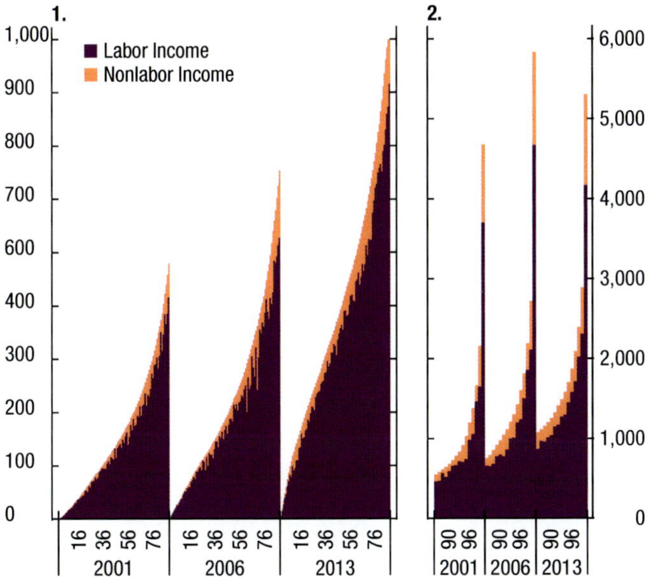

Sources: INE??? Bolivia; and IMF staff calculations.
[1]The distributions show the monthly household income per capita in real terms (2000). Panel 1: 1st to 85th percentile; Panel 2: 86th to 100th percentile.

Figure 23. Bolivia: Index of Monthly Real Labor Income by Educational Level
(Index: 2001 = 100)

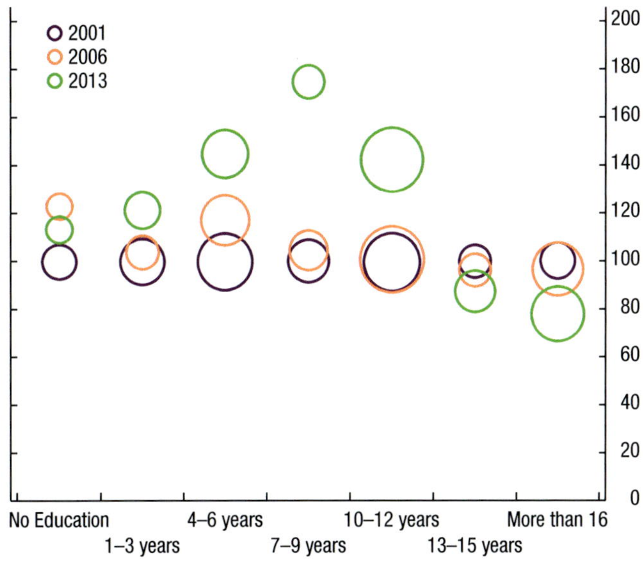

Sources: Bolivia's household surveys (MECOVI); and IMF staff calculations.
Note: The size of the bubble corresponds to the relative size of workers in each category.

Figure 24. Real Labor per Capita and Sectorial Employment in Bolivia, 2006–13

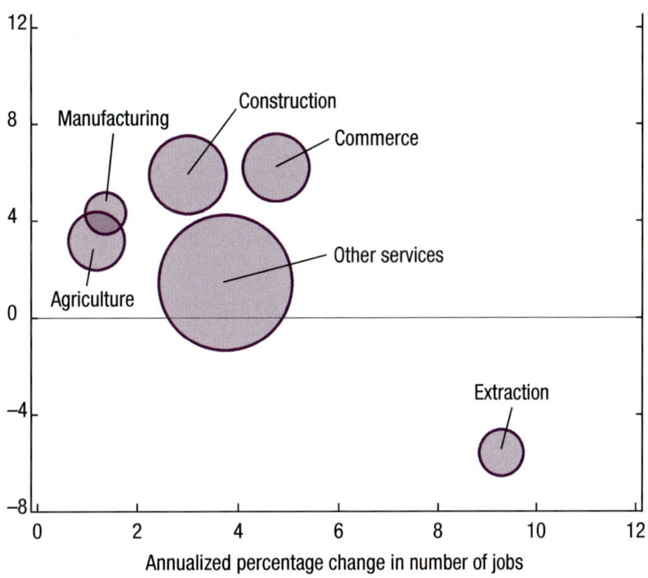

Sources: Bolivia's household surveys (MECOVI); and IMF staff calculations.
Note: The size of the bubble corresponds to the relative size of workers in each category.

Decomposing the Reduction in Inequality and Poverty in Bolivia

In this section we formalize the discussion of the key drivers of poverty and inequality reduction in Bolivia. The so-called Shapley decomposition largely confirms the above conclusions.

We use the method described in Azevedo, Inchauste, and Sanfelice (2013). They proposed a Shapley-Shorrocks decomposition that corrects path dependence in the standard Barros and others (2006) calculation.[3] The method is simple; first, it divides real household income per capita from the household survey into j components (for example, household income per capita = household non-labor income per capita + household labor income per capita in sector A + household labor income per capita in sector B, etc.) and chooses two years to compare a poverty or inequality indicator.

$$Y_{Hpc} = Y_{Hpc,1} + Y_{Hpc,2} + \ldots + Y_{Hpc,j}$$

Selected indicators are constructed based on Y_{Hpc}. Let ϑ be any measure of inequality or poverty, and $F(.)$ be the cumulative density function of household income per capita:

$$\vartheta = \varnothing(F(Y_{Hpc,1}, Y_{Hpc,2}, \ldots, Y_{Hpc,j}))$$

Then, the method essentially alters the distribution of total household income per capita in the latter year by replacing every component of the distribution by data from the same component in the former year in any possible order. After that, a counterfactual inequality/poverty indicator is calculated with that new distribution to obtain:

$$\tilde{\vartheta} = \varnothing(F(Y_{Hpc,1}, Y_{Hpc,2}, \ldots, \tilde{Y}_{Hpc,j}))$$

Then, the contributions can be calculated in the following way:

$\mu_0 = \varnothing(F(Y_{Hpc,1}, Y_{Hpc,2}, \ldots, Y_{Hpc,j}))$ Initial Inequality/Poverty Rate

$\tilde{\mu}_1 = \varnothing(F(\tilde{Y}_{Hpc,1}, Y_{Hpc,2}, \ldots, Y_{Hpc,j}))$ Contribution of Component 1 = $\tilde{\mu}_1 - \mu_0$

$\tilde{\mu}_2 = \varnothing(F(\tilde{Y}_{Hpc,1}, \tilde{Y}_{Hpc,2}, \ldots, Y_{Hpc,j}))$ Contribution of Component 2 = $\tilde{\mu}_2 - \tilde{\mu}_1$

. . . .

$\tilde{\mu}_j = \varnothing(F(\tilde{Y}_{Hpc,1}, \tilde{Y}_{Hpc,2}, \ldots, \tilde{Y}_{Hpc,j}))$ Contribution of Component j = $\tilde{\mu}_j - \tilde{\mu}_{j-1}$

[3]There are some important methodological issues and associated caveats to note when using Shapley decompositions (see Sastre and Trannoy 2002).

Figure 25. Bolivia: Decomposition of Reductions in Poverty and Inequality by Education Level

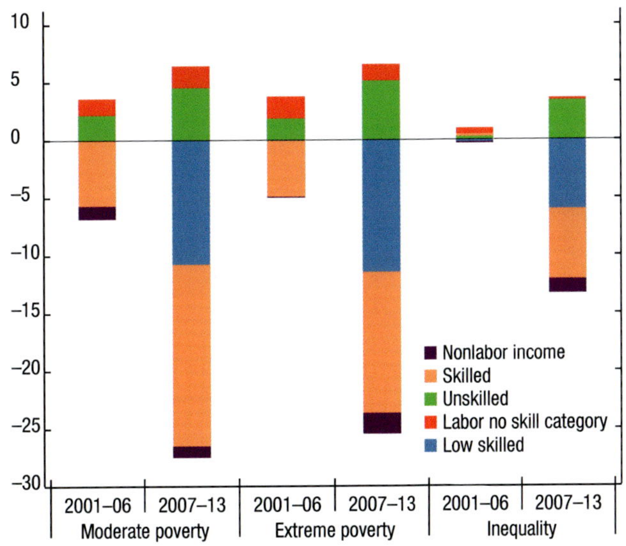

Source: IMF staff calculations using Bolivia's Household Surveys.
Note: Gini coefficient change based on re-scaled gini coefficients in the range (0–100).

Table 3. Bolivia: Composition of Household Income per Capita

	2001	2002	2006	2007	2011	2012	2013
Labor	83.6	84.7	82.8	82.4	81.8	80.9	79.1
Nonlabor	15.6	14.5	16.4	17.0	17.9	18.4	20.4
Returns of Capital	*0.2*	*0.3*	*0.2*	*0.1*	*0.2*	*0.1*	
Transfers from Government	*5.9*	*5.4*	*5.7*	*5.4*	*9.8*	*11.2*	
Transfers between households	*9.4*	*8.8*	*10.5*	*11.5*	*7.8*	*7.1*	

Source: IMF staff calculations based on Bolivia's Household Surveys (ENAHO)

Since the order in which the cumulative effects are calculated matters, this process repeats for each possible path. Finally, the average effect of each component represents the contribution of it to the change in the indicator of interest.

The results indicate that while higher government transfers had a positive effect, the bulk of the improvement is explained by labor income variations (Figure 25). This is perhaps not surprising given Table 3 shows that, throughout the boom period, labor income accounted for about 80 percent of household income, even though the role of transfers increased significantly. Mechanically, movements in labor income thus have a bigger impact on total income than do movements in transfers. But of course, if transfers are well-targeted the Shapley result is still not immediately obvious ex ante.

Figure 26. Bolivia: Further Decomposition of Reductions in Poverty and Inequality

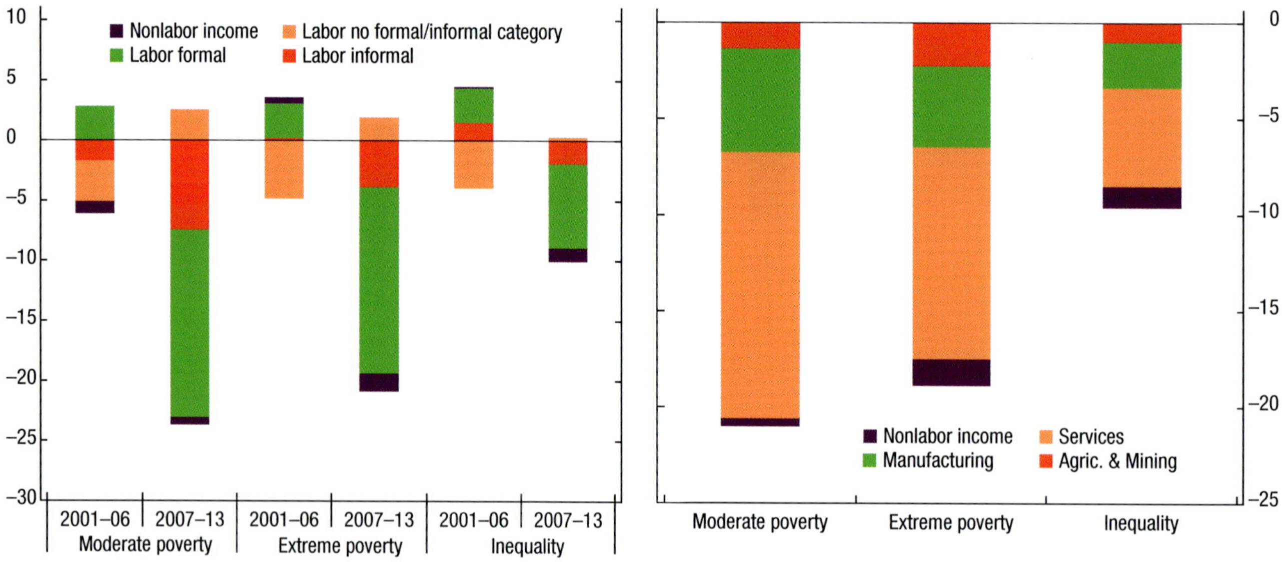

Source: IMF staff calculations using Bolivia's Household Surveys.

The results emanating from the Shapley decompositions will be corroborated in Chapter 4. Specifically, the model results will show that in the case of Bolivia, the commodity price boom, the increase in skills among the working population, and migration from rural to urban centers can account for about two-third of the fall in the Gini coefficient in the period 2006–13. These changes would have led to a decrease in inequality passing through an increase in labor income, especially for the low skilled, and a consequent reduction of the skill premium.

Additional decompositions show that jobs in the formal and services sectors contributed most to inequality and poverty reduction. Figure 26 highlights the role of formal sector employment in the socioeconomic improvements, with only a small contribution from the informal sector.[4] Finally, Figure 26 also shows that the largest contribution to poverty reduction came from the services sector.

[4]On average, labor income per capita in the informal sector represented about 60 percent of its corresponding figure in the formal sector.

Figure 27. Poverty Reduction and Change in Employment Composition in Bolivia
(Kernel density, 2001–12)

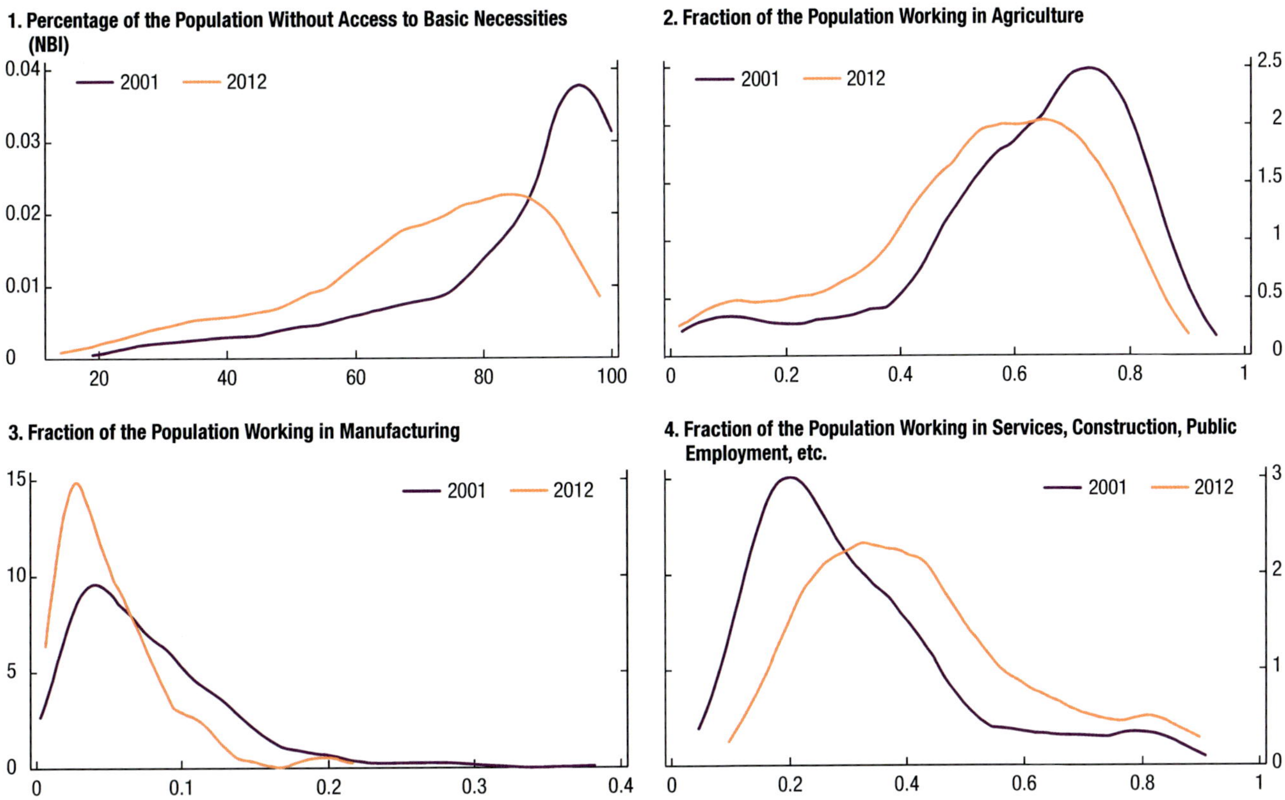

Source: IMF staff calculations using Bolivia's Populaiton Census.

The Impact of the Resource Boom at the Local Level

Empirical Strategy

To understand the change Bolivia went through in the boom years from a different angle, we turn to local level census data. The main advantage of census data in this context is that it can be used at any desirable level of geographic disaggregation. Household survey data, on the other hand, is not representative at the municipal level.[5] Figure 27 gives a flavor of the census data at the municipal level and the progress the whole of Bolivia experienced between the 2001 and 2012 census waves. Poverty decreased across the country—the whole distribution of average municipal level poverty shifted to

[5]The census-based poverty measure is somewhat different from the household survey one given that the Bolivian census does not provide income information. The census-based measure is constructed by looking at the percentage of the population without access to basic necessities (sanitation, water, electricity, adequate living space, etc.). See Feres and Mancero (2001).

the left (toward less poverty) over the period. The figure also shows that the share of employment in the nontradable sectors (services, construction, public employment, etc.) increased considerably. This appears to be consistent with earlier results which showed a strong expansion of the services sector.

To test for the impact of the natural resource boom at the local level, we estimate the following simple difference in difference regression model using data from the 2001 and 2012 population census

$$y_{it} = \alpha + \gamma EM_i + \theta T_t + \rho(EM_i * T_t) + X_{it}^{``}\beta + \varepsilon_{it}$$

where y_{it} is the dependent variable, EM_i is a dummy variable which is 1 for extractive sector municipalities, T_t is a time dummy which is 1 in 2012 and the interaction $D_{it} = (EM_i * T_t)$ is the treatment variable, so that ρ is our coefficient of interest. $X_{it}^{``}$ is a vector of municipality and time-varying covariates. We will differentiate between mineral producers, "small" oil and gas producers and the natural gas megacampo producers.[6]

Since data prior to 2001 are not available for Bolivia, the parallel trend assumption or control for pretreatment trends in the estimation cannot be explicitly tested. To improve identification, the control group is limited to those municipalities that have the best covariate overlap with the treatment group. In other words, the aim is to compare extractive sector municipalities to municipalities that prior to the resource boom looked very similar to them. To do this, an entropy balancing technique is used (Hainmueller and Xu 2013). The method assigns weights between 0 and 1 to municipalities in the control group to achieve optimal covariance overlap and is well suited to the setup with many more control municipalities than treatment municipalities.[7]

Results

Both mining and hydrocarbon production significantly reduced poverty in producing municipalities and also led to some reallocation of labor (see Figure 28, panel 1). In mineral mining municipalities, poverty fell by about 4 percentage points (relative to other Bolivian municipalities). They additionally experienced a reduction in agricultural employment and increases in

[6]Production of natural gas is concentrated in the southern province of Tarija, while mining has traditionally been located in the highlands of Potosi and Oruro. Out of a total of 339 municipalities, there are 48 which produce either metal or hydrocarbons (extractive sector municipalities) in Bolivia. 24 produce hydrocarbons and 24 produce metals. See Toscani (2017) for additional details.

[7]Entropy balancing achieves virtually perfect overlap both for the first and the second moment of the distribution. Like the now-popular synthetic control method, entropy balancing implicitly makes a strong linearity assumption, however. An alternative that could be explored in future work is to exclude municipalities that are adjacent to resource municipalities to alleviate concerns about spillovers.

Figure 28. Bolivia: Impact of Natural Resource Boom on Extractive Sector Municipalities
(Kernel density, 2001–12)

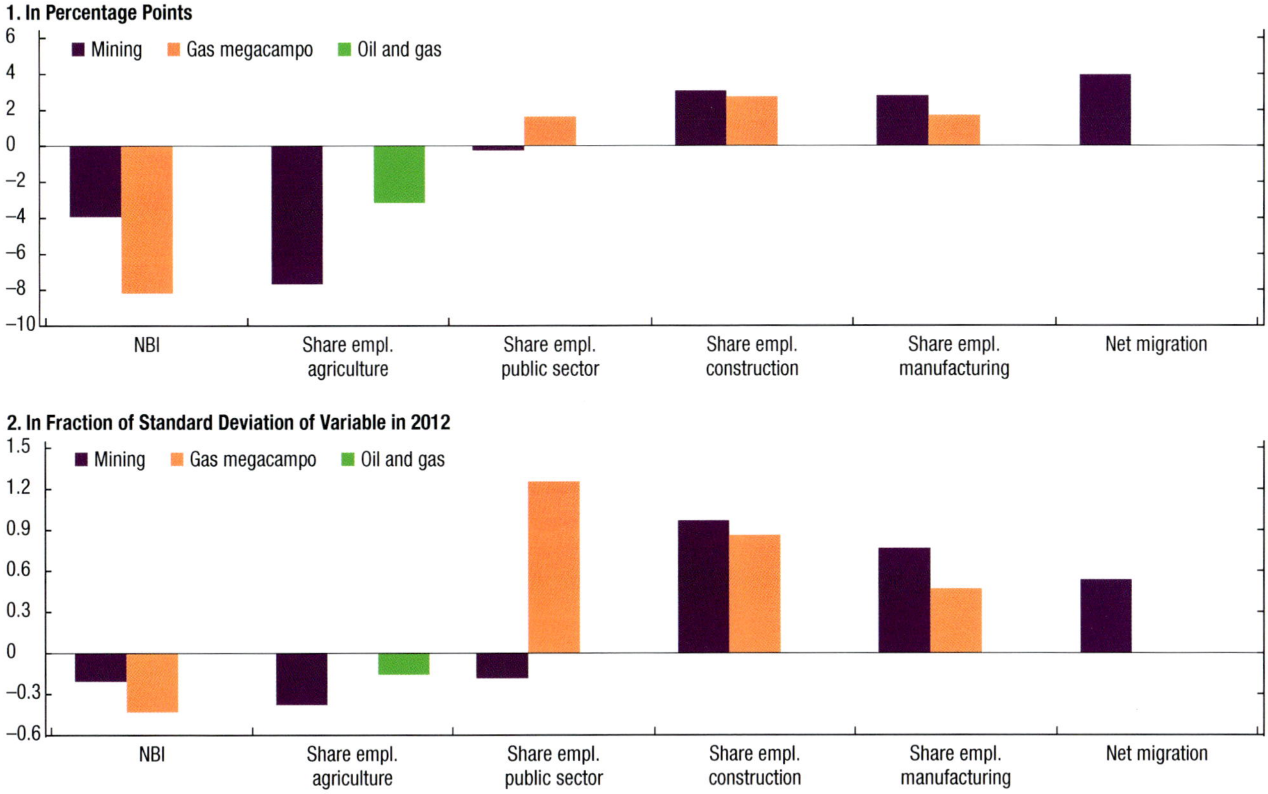

Source: IMF staff calculations using Bolivia's Population Census.
Note: NBI = unsatisfied basic needs.

construction and manufacturing employment as well as higher net migration. Municipalities with gas megacampos, on the other hand, experienced double the fall in poverty (8 percentage points) relative to metal municipalities and no fall in agricultural employment or increase in net migration. At the same time, they also experienced an increase in the share of employment in public sector administration by roughly 2 percentage points, suggesting that fiscal windfall might have been used for public employment. Other oil and gas municipalities, without large discoveries, did not experience any significant impact.

Figure 28, panel 2, puts the magnitude of the estimated coefficients into context by scaling them with the standard deviation of the respective dependent variable. This highlights just how large the increase in public sector administration was in megacampo municipalities. The coefficient suggests that the share of public sector employment increased by over one standard deviation.

Similarly, the increase in construction employment in both gas and mineral municipalities is large (close to 0.9 standard deviations). The reduction in poverty, evaluated in this way, seems less impressive, however, at only 0.2 and 0.4 standard deviations, respectively.

To shed more light on the mechanisms underlying these results, it is insightful to consider some salient differences between how metal municipalities and gas municipalities were affected during the boom. A first important difference is the relative labor intensity of mining and gas production, with the former being significantly more labor intensive. On average, in mining municipalities, the share of workers employed in mining is close to 20 percent, while in gas municipalities the share of workers employed in gas production is only about 3 percent. An increase in metal production (as observed in Bolivia as a consequence of higher prices) thus has a much bigger impact on direct labor demand than an increase in gas production.

The second important difference is that municipalities with gas megacampos received a significantly larger fiscal windfall than metal municipalities. In 2012 total fiscal revenues from mineral mining were about 1 percent of GDP, half of which were royalties that are redistributed exclusively to producing departments and municipalities. In the same year, total fiscal revenues from hydrocarbons were above 10 percent of GDP—of which about half was distributed to subnational governments.

To note just how big the fiscal windfall was, consider the departmental budget breakdown of Bolivia for 2012 (Figure 29).[8] The main gas region (Tarija) has a population share of about 5 percent. Yet its budget accounted for over a third of all departmental revenues and wages, and nearly half of all departmental capital expenditure. The largest part of Tarija's revenues stems from hydrocarbon taxes and royalties directly related to its role as the major producer in Bolivia (roughly 70 percent of total Bolivian gas production at the time). While most of these revenues accrue at the departmental level, Tarija pays 45 percent of its hydrocarbon royalties directly to the semi-autonomous region of Gran Chaco, where a population of roughly 150,000 people thus ends up with an estimated 7 percent of all of Bolivia's hydrocarbon revenues—somewhat below 1 percent of national GDP.

And yet, Tarija suffered from severe fiscal imbalances immediately after the end of the commodity boom, highlighting the difficulty of managing revenue volatility at the subnational level, an important challenge even at the national level.

[8]Ideally, we would have explored the detailed impact of the boom on municipal fiscal revenues (similar to the analysis done for Brazil). Unfortunately, the necessary data was not available.

Figure 29. Departmental Budgets in Bolivia, 2012
(USD per capita)

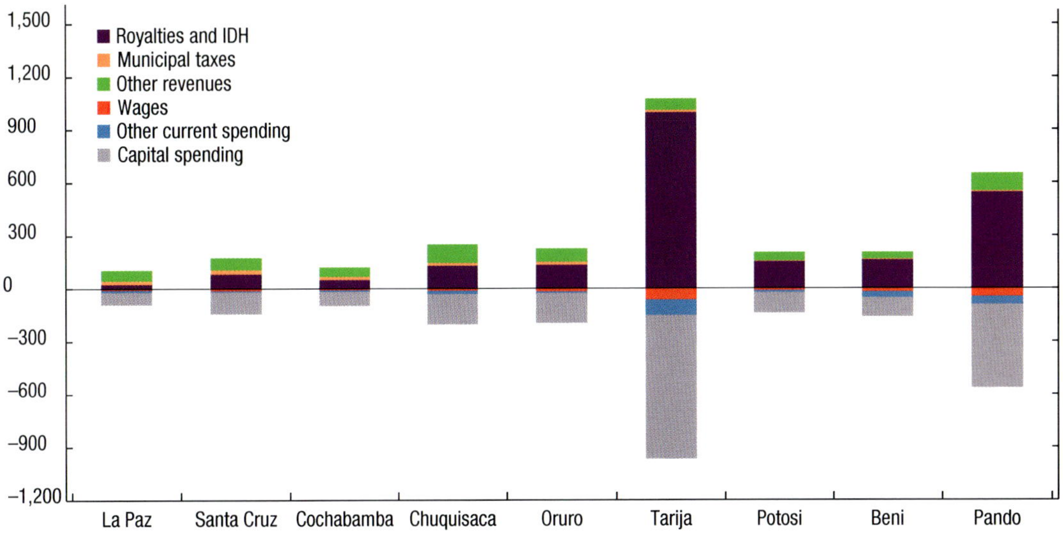

Sources: National authorities; and IMF staff calculations.
Note: IDH = direct hydrocarbon tax.

As the case studies for Brazil and Peru will show, several of the Bolivia results seem to hold more broadly. The important role of increased labor income in an expanding nontradable sector in explaining lower poverty and inequality is a recurring theme as are the problems associated with a large fiscal windfall at the subnational level.

Brazil

Overview of Extractive Sector in Brazil

Brazil is a not only a large, diversified economy but also one of the main mineral producers globally, as well as a major oil and gas producer. Brazil is one of the largest producers of iron ore, aluminums, and bauxite and an important producer of other metals such as gold and copper. Brazil also has important (mainly offshore) oil reserves and achieved self-sufficiency in 2006. The country was thus a major beneficiary of the commodity price boom, with its terms of trade for goods improving by 24 percent between 2000 and 2010 (20 percent between 2000 and 2014).

Production of natural resources is regionally concentrated, creating a relatively small group of municipalities with very high per capita natural resource production. The main offshore oil fields are concentrated off the coast of Rio de Janeiro, while most onshore production (which nowadays is of a significantly smaller magnitude) is concentrated in the northeast and Amazon regions. Mineral mining occurs mainly in the interior state of Minas Gerais as well as the Amazon region. Out of Brazil's 5,565 municipalities, the top 20 producers concentrate 75 percent of total production.

Brazil collects royalties on both mineral and onshore and offshore hydrocarbon production, with an important share of royalties accruing to producing municipalities.[9] For oil and gas, the allocation formula is complex but implies that for the major producer municipalities revenues from oil can account for as much as 50 percent of their income.

Stylized Facts on Inequality, Poverty, and Natural Resource Production in Brazil

As mentioned previously, in line with most of Latin America, poverty and inequality in Brazil fell strongly during the resource boom years. The Gini coefficient fell by 7 basis points, from 0.6 to 0.53, during the 2000s, close to the average reduction in inequality for LAC-18 (see Lustig, Lopez-Calva, and Ortiz-Juarez 2013), while according to national data the poverty rate fell from 28 percent to 14 percent.[10] During the commodity price boom period, average real income growth was high in Brazil for all but the top decile of the income distribution (see Goes and Karpowicz 2017), mirroring results in Bolivia and LAC more broadly.

How Does the Literature Explain the Fall in Poverty and Inequality in Brazil During the Commodity Boom?

Several authors have exploited household income data to try and understand the drivers of the fall in poverty and inequality in Brazil. Barros and others (2010) estimate that the fall in inequality between 2001 and 2007 was driven both by an expansion in government transfers and a compression in the ratio of labor income of better educated workers relative to those less-educated. They explain the latter by an expansion in the supply of educated workers. Goes and Karpowicz (2017) find that most of the change in the Gini can be explained by labor income growth, higher schooling levels and labor formalization, but the targeted social program, *Bolsa Família*, also contributed to income convergence.

[9]Brazil is a federal country with three layers of government: federal, state, and municipal.
[10]Source: Brazilian Institute of Geography and Economics (IBGE).

Azevedo, Inchauste, and Sanfelice (2013) use Shapley decompositions to explain the role of different factors in reducing inequality in several Latin American countries, while Azevedo and others (2013) use the same approach to explain the reduction in poverty. For Brazil, they find that the largest contributor to lower income inequality was higher labor income (contribution of 45 percent). At the same time though, government transfers (contribution of 20 percent) and pensions (contribution of 18 percent) also played an important role. Similarly, for poverty, employment and earnings growth was the largest single factor, but nonlabor income (notably government transfers) played a very important role, more so than in a number of other Latin American countries. The importance of transfers in Brazil can be noted by observing that the share of transfers in total household income of the bottom 20 percent of the distribution went from 3 percent to 24 percent between 2000 and 2010 (Azevedo, Inchauste, and Sanfelice 2013).

The Impact of the Resource Boom at the Local Level

Empirical Strategy

As in the case of Bolivia, we use census data for the local level analysis.[11] Figure 30 shows the progress Brazil made between the last two census rounds by plotting municipal-level distributions of income per capita, poverty, inequality, and informality in 2000 and 2010. The income per capita distribution shifted to the right, indicating higher income per capita in most municipalities. At the same time, poverty decreased across the board, inequality fell, and labor formality increased to some degree. The bimodal distribution for poverty and other variables is testimony to the large regional disparities in Brazil.

The Brazilian data are very rich and allows us to calculate the *per capita* value of natural resource production by year and municipality.[12] Looking at Figure 31 we see that while the majority of municipalities produce very little to no natural resources per capita, more than 250 municipalities produce more than 1,000 real per capita (which compares to annual per capita income of about 6,000 real in the average municipality in 2010). 66 municipalities produced over 15,000 real per capita worth of natural resources in 2010 and

[11]We combine data from a number of sources in the analysis. Municipal-level data on poverty, income, inequality, income, and employment by sector comes from the 2000 and 2010 rounds of the population census provided by the Brazilian Institute of Geography and Economics (IBGE). Data on mineral production and mineral royalties by municipality are taken from the Brazilian Mining Ministry (DNPM). Oil royalties data by municipality is taken from the oil and gas regulator (ANP). Data on oil production by field are taken from ANP. It is then mapped to municipalities using information on geographic location of fields and municipalities. Municipal fiscal data comes from Ipeadata.

[12]The per capita number should be the more relevant measure than the total value when thinking about determinants of poverty and inequality.

Figure 30. Municipality Level Distributions of Income, Poverty, Inequality, and Informality in Brazil from the 2000 and 2010 Census
(Kernel Density)

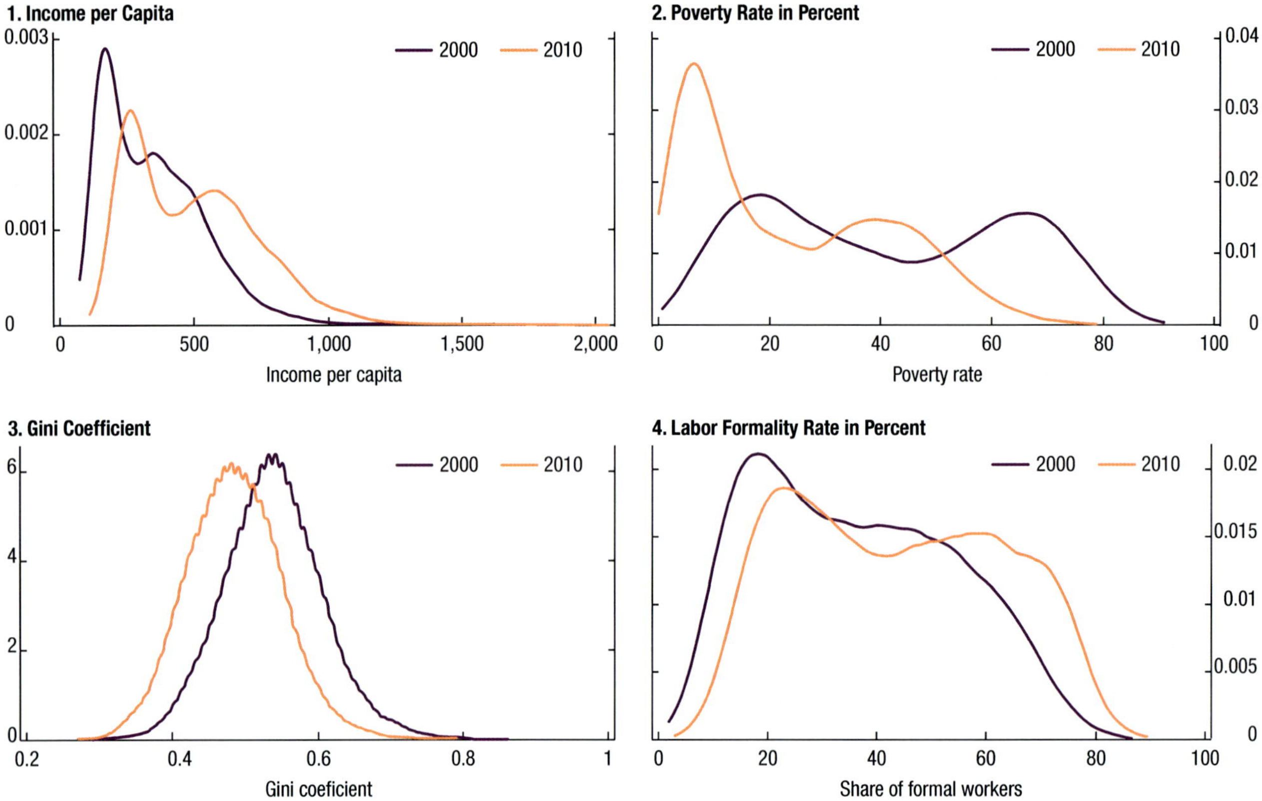

Sources: Brazilian Institute for Geography and Economics (IBGE) population census; and IMF staff calculations.
Note: The panels in the figure show the distribution of income per capita, poverty, Gini index, and labor formality for the 5,565 Brazilian municipalities in 2000 and 2010. Poverty is defined as a monthly income below 140 reals. The bimodal distribution of income, poverty, and formality is testimony to the vast difference in development levels between Brazilian regions. The north and northeast are significantly poorer than the south.

10 municipalities produced more than 100,000 real per capita (depending on the exchange rate, about $30,000). Those "mega-producers" include Parauapebas in the state of Para, the location of one of the largest iron ore mines in the world, as well as Campos dos Goytacazes in Rio de Janeiro state, which faces Brazil's main offshore oil fields.

The value of per capita production increased significantly during the boom period.[13] Table 4 shows key summary statistics for the change in the value of production. As expected, we can note that on average the value of per capita production (in 2010 Brazilian real) increased over the period, driven by

[13]For mineral production, the earliest data we have is 2004. The value for 2000 is assumed to be the same as the one in 2004. This might bias our results to some degree but it should bias them against finding an impact, given that the change in the value of production was likely larger between 2000–10 than 2004–10.

Figure 31. Value of Natural Resource Production in Brazilian Municipalities, 2010
(Per capita, in 2010 Brazilian real)

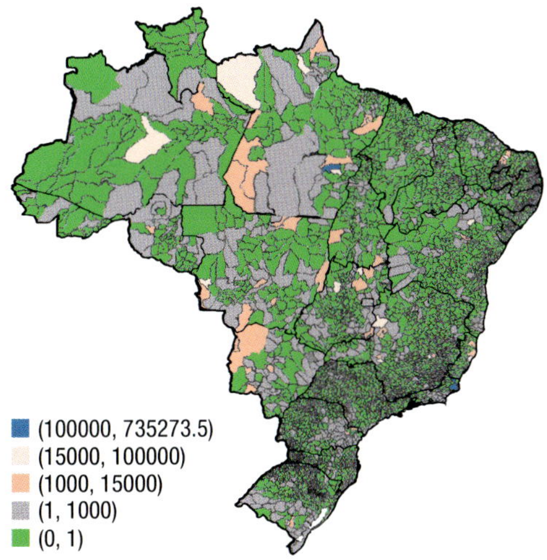

Sources: Agencia Nacional de Petroleo (ANP); Brazilian Institute for Geography and Economics (IBGE) population census; and IMF staff calculations.
Note: The map shows natural resource (hydrocarbons + minerals) production per capita in 2010 for the 5,565 Brazilian municipalities. Population data are from the 2010 population census. Data on hydrocarbon production volumes by field are from Agencia Nacional de Petroleo (ANP). It is then distributed to municipalities based on geographic information and converted into values using annual price data by state also from ANP (see Appendix). Mineral production values data are from the Brazilian Mining Ministry. Values are in constant 2010 Brazilian real.

Table 4. Change in Value of Natural Resource Production and Natural Resource Revenues in Brazilian Municipalities, 2000–10 (per capita, in constant 2010 Brazilian Real)

Variable	Obs	Mean	Std. Dev.	Min	Max
Natural resource production	5,565	285	13,824	−148,455	705,960
Hydrocarbon production	5,565	184	10,812	−148,455	705,960
Onshore hydrocarbon production	5,565	−21	973	−38,809	24,411
Offshore hydrocarbon production	5,565	205	10,765	−148,455	705,960
Mineral production	5,565	101	8,650	−140,951	392,654
Natural resource royalties	5,565	15	290	−3,152	14,312
Hydrocarbon royalties	5,565	13	246	−3,152	14,312
Mining royalties	5,565	2	158	−2,540	7,265

Sources: IMF staff calculations, Brazilian Institute of Geography and Statistics (IBGE), Agencia Nacional de Petroleo (ANP), and the Brazilian Mining Ministry.
Note: All value refer to the change in the per capita value between 2000 and 2010. Values are in constant 2010 Brazilian Real

offshore oil and mineral production, while on average the value of onshore oil production contracted slightly. The standard deviation is very high, providing the variation that can be exploited in the empirical analysis. It is also worth pointing out that natural resource royalties increased together with the value of production, leading to increased royalty revenues of several thou-

Table 5. Impact of Natural Resource Boom on Producer Municipalities in Brazil

Brazil	Poverty	Gini Coefficient
Impact of increase in real per capita natural resource production (range for top 20 increases)	−0.39*** to −9.1***	0 to −0.05**
Impact of being a natural resource producer municipality (dummy variable analysis)	−1.44***	0

Source: IMF staff calculations.
Note: The first row of the table shows the product of the estimated coefficient with the real per capita production of the top 20 producer municipalities. $^{*}p < 0.10$; $^{**}p < 0.005$; $^{***}p < 0.01$.

sand US dollars per capita in some cases (real–dollar exchange rate was about 2 to 1 in 2010).

To capture the impact of the resource boom on local poverty and inequality we estimate the following equation:

$$\Delta y_{i,2010} = \alpha + \beta \Delta x_{i,2010} + \gamma \Delta y_{i,2000} + \delta y_{i,2000} + \theta_s + \rho Z_i + \epsilon_i$$

where $\Delta y_{i,2010}$ is the change in the dependent variable between 2000 and 2010 in municipality i and $\Delta x_{i,2010}$ is the change in the explanatory variable (natural resource production per capita measured in constant 2010 Brazilian real) in municipality i. β is the coefficient of interest. We include both the level of the dependent variable in 2000 ($y_{i,2000}$) to capture convergence effects as well as the change in the dependent variable between the previous census rounds (1991 to 2000 – $\Delta y_{i,2000}$) to control for municipality-specific trends. Additionally, we include state fixed effects θ_s to account for regional dynamics and a vector of geographic controls Z_i which measure whether a municipality is located on the coast, for example. Standard errors are clustered at the state level.

Results

Higher real values of natural resource production are associated with larger declines in poverty, with producer municipalities reducing poverty by 1.4 percentage points on average relative to nonproducer ones (Table 5). Regarding inequality, the results are mixed, with statistical significance depending on which technique is used. This is consistent with the earlier cross-country results of a clearer result on the poverty front.

To discriminate between the fiscal channel and the direct employment channel of the resource boom, we separate natural resources into offshore hydrocarbons and minerals.[14] We start by illustrating that the fiscal windfall channel is present for both offshore oil and minerals but that the direct

[14]Onshore oil production is also included in the regressions but since it is never found to be significant results are not reported to not clutter the tables. Recalling Table 2 shows why onshore oil production is not found to have any impact—the value of onshore oil production on average did not change between 2000 and 2010, in fact it slightly contracted as old fields were slowly winding down production. The level of royalties from onshore production is also a magnitude smaller than those from offshore.

Table 6. Brazil: Impact of Mineral and Offshore Hydrocarbon Production on Municipal Revenues and Extractive Sector Employment

VARIABLES	(1) Natural Resource Royalties per Capita	(2) (Current) Revenues per Capita	(3) Share of Workers in Extractive Industries
Change in mineral production per capita	0.0174***	0.0241***	1.33e-05***
	(0.000922)	(0.00601)	(4.19e-06)
Change in offshore oil and gas production per capita	0.0209***	0.0248***	−2.56-e06
	(0.00130)	(0.00264)	(1.82e-06)
Geography controls	Yes	Yes	Yes
Dependent variable in 2000	Yes	Yes	Yes
Change in dependent variable between 1991–2000	No	No	No
State fixed effects	Yes	Yes	Yes
Observations	5,507	4,982	5,507
R-squared	0.886	0.834	0.223

Source: IMF staff calculations.
Note: All dependent variables are specified as the change between 2000 and 2010.

employment channel is only present for minerals (Table 6). Columns 1 and 2 of Table 6 show that both the mineral as well as the hydrocarbon boom led to a fiscal windfall. Column 1 indicates that for every Brazilian real of mineral production, royalty revenues increase by 1.74 cents, while for every real of offshore oil production, royalty revenues increase by about 2 cents. Column 2 shows that overall municipal current revenues increase by more than just royalties—for both offshore oil and minerals, revenues increase by about 2.4 cents for every Real of production. Below we will explore the fiscal aspects in more detail.

Column 3 of Table 6 shows that although mineral production significantly increases the share of workers in the extractive sector, offshore oil and gas production does not. Oil and gas production is a capital-intensive but labor-scarce activity. In the case of offshore production this is amplified, given that offshore oil and gas production does not take place directly in a municipality but off the coast, so that there is no direct onshore employment, or indeed investment, effect. Even when the workers are not on the oil platform, they might live somewhere completely different from the municipality which faces the platform. Mineral production, on the other hand, is always onshore, and is more labor intensive than oil and gas production.[15]

Figure 32 shows that the mineral boom reduced poverty and led to labor reallocation. Poverty fell, labor formality increased, and labor shifted from agriculture and manufacturing into construction and services. In terms of quantification, the effects are small for most municipalities—a one standard deviation increase in the value of mineral production per capita reduces the poverty rate by only 0.2 percentage points, for example. For the big producers, however, the impacts are economically highly significant—with

[15]The argument extends to general backward linkages (that is, demand for non-labor inputs) and not only labor demand.

Figure 32. Brazil: Impact of Natural Resource Extraction on Poverty and Employment

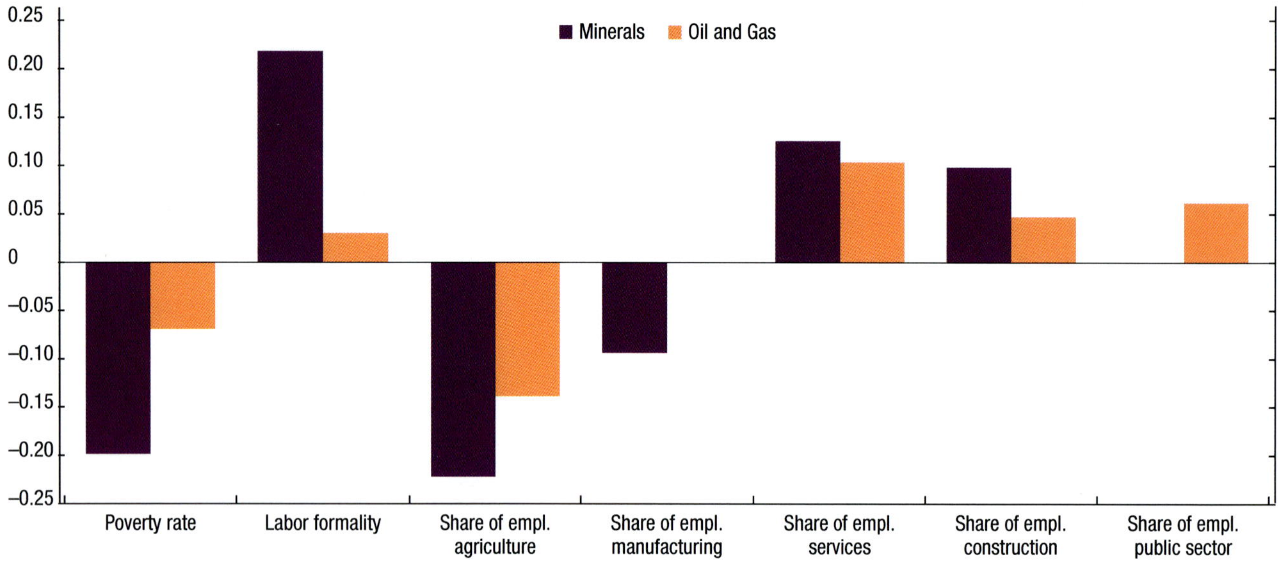

Sources: Brazilian Institute of Geography and Statistics (IBGE); and IMF staff calculations.
Note: All dependent variables are specified as the change between the 2000 and 2010 census. The change between the 1991 and 2000 census is included in the regressions as a control variable when available. Standard errors are clustered at the state level. Estimated coefficients are set to zero when they are not significant at least at the 10 percent level. When they are significantly different from zero, the graph shows the impact of a one standard deviation increase in the value of natural resource production per capita between 2000 and 2010.

estimated reductions in poverty of between 3 and 9 percentage points for the top 5 producers.

The impact of the offshore oil boom on poverty and labor allocation was much smaller. In contrast to mineral municipalities but in line with the results for Bolivia, public sector employment rose in offshore oil municipalities. Labor also shifts toward services and construction—since there is no direct employment effect (see Table 6) and no investment boom given the offshore location, these effects must be purely due to an increase in public expenditure tied to the fiscal windfall.

Table 7 shows more details on the fiscal channel, illustrating that it works very similarly in mineral and offshore hydrocarbon municipalities, but with some subtle differences. Columns 1 and 2 repeat the results of Table 7—overall revenues increase by about 2.4 cents for every real of natural resource production in both mineral and oil municipalities. However, the composition of the increase is a little different between the two. While royalties increase less in mineral municipalities, tax revenues increase by more. And when looking at exactly which municipal tax revenues drive the increase, we see that it is the municipal tax on services (ISS–Column 6). The fiscal data thus

Table 7. Brazil: Impact of Natural Resource Extraction on Municipal Revenues and Expenditures

	REVENUES						
VARIABLES	(1) Current Revenues	(2) Natural Resource Royalties	(3) Transfer Revenues	(4) Tax Revenues	(5) IPTU	(6) ISS	(7) Other Taxes
Change in mineral production per capita	0.0241*** (0.00601)	0.0174*** (0.000922)	0.0218*** (0.00525)	0.00177*** (0.000575)	3.61e-05** (1.49e-05)	0.00169*** (0.000560)	2.49e-05 (8.14e-05)
Change in offshore oil and gas production per capita	0.0248*** (0.00264)	0.0209*** (0.00130)	0.0233*** (0.00251)	0.000462** (0.000195)	−1.57e-06 (2.09e-05)	0.000293* (0.000158)	0.000131** (5.15e-05)
Observations	4,982	5,507	4,982	4,982	4,982	4,982	4,982
R-squared	0.834	0.886	0.849	0.065	0.451	0.064	0.100

	EXPENDITURES			
VARIABLES	(8) Current Expenditure	(9) Transfer Expenditures	(10) Wage Expenditures	(11) Capital Spending
Change in mineral production per capita	0.00549*** (0.00129)	0.000161 (0.000106)	0.00262** (0.00117)	0.00868*** (0.00181)
Change in offshore oil and gas production per capita	0.00688*** (0.000437)	0.000663*** (0.000169)	0.00370*** (0.000335)	0.00543*** (0.000619)
Observations	4,982	4,982	4,982	4,982
R-squared	0.942	0.959	0.693	0.489

Source: IMF staff calculations.
Note: All dependent variables are specified as the change between the 2000 and 2010 census. IPTU = property tax; ISS = municipal tax on services

corroborate the expansion of the services sector as a positive spillover from the boom in the commodity sector in mineral municipalities.[16]

On the expenditure side, both mineral royalties and oil royalties are not supposed to be spent on interest payments and wages. But wage payments do increase with mineral and oil production. Studying the impact of offshore oil royalties in Brazil, Caselli and Michaels (2013) find that royalties lead municipalities to report higher spending, but the results in terms of various measures of well-being were modest, raising some concerns about the ultimate effectiveness of the fiscal windfall at the local level.

Peru

Overview of Extractive Sector in Peru

Peru has historically been a metal exporter and expanded its commodity export portfolio with oil and natural gas exports in the mid-2000s (Figure 33). Extractive industries represented close to 14 percent of GDP on average over our period of study (2007–11). Peru's largest commodity exports over those years were gold, copper, and oil (including natural gas). Notwithstanding important growth in hydrocarbons production during the last 10

[16]Property taxes (IPTU) also increase significantly, but the magnitude is much smaller than for services taxes.

Figure 33. Peru: Value of Exports
(Millions of $US)

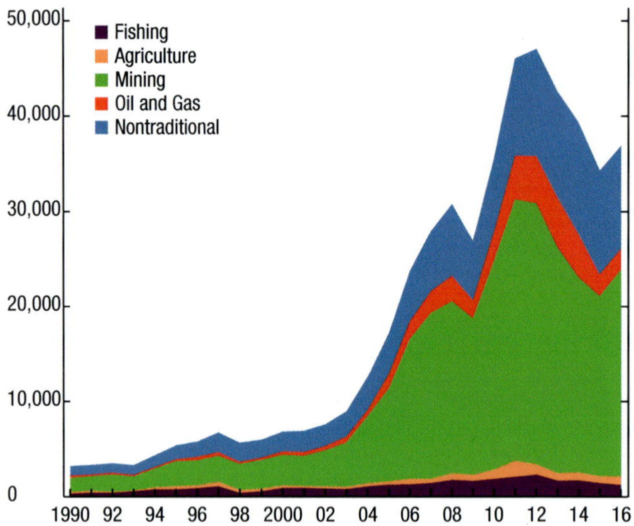

Sources: National authorities; and IMF staff calculations.
Note: The non-traditional category includes some agricultural exports that grew strongly.

Figure 34. Peru: Mining, Oil, and Gas Canon
(Millions of Soles)

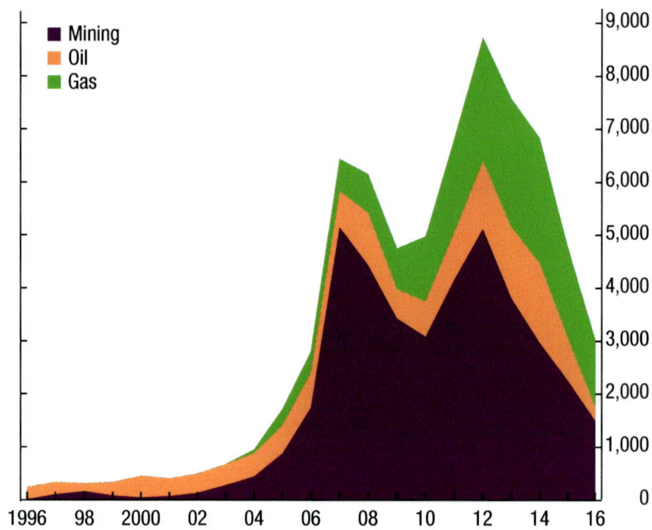

Sources: National authorities; and IMF staff calculations.

years, metal exports were seven times larger over the period 2007–11. The price index of Peru's exports improved by 44 percent during those years, and the terms of trade increased by 13 percent. The volume of exports grew by 15 percent.

While natural resource rents are collected at the central government level, an important share is transferred back to local governments (Figure 34). The mechanism to distribute the funds is constituted by the so-called *canons* which have slightly different rules across sectors and aim to decentralize resource windfalls. For instance, with regard to the mining and gas sectors, the central government transfers 50 percent of the taxes levied on mining/gas companies to local governments in producing regions. In the case of the oil canon, the transfer is equal to 12.5 percent of the production value. The importance of canon/royalty transfers varies across regions (Figure 35) but in some departments they represent close to 90 percent of total per capita transfers received (for example, Moquegua, Cusco).

Stylized Facts on Income, Inequality, and Poverty in Peru

Inequality in Peru dropped significantly during the commodity boom. During our period of analysis (2007–11), the Gini coefficient fell by 6 basis points, from 0.51 to 0.45, based on the World Bank SEDLAC harmonized

Figure 35. Peru: Transfers to Departments, 2007–11
(Percent and soles in right scale)

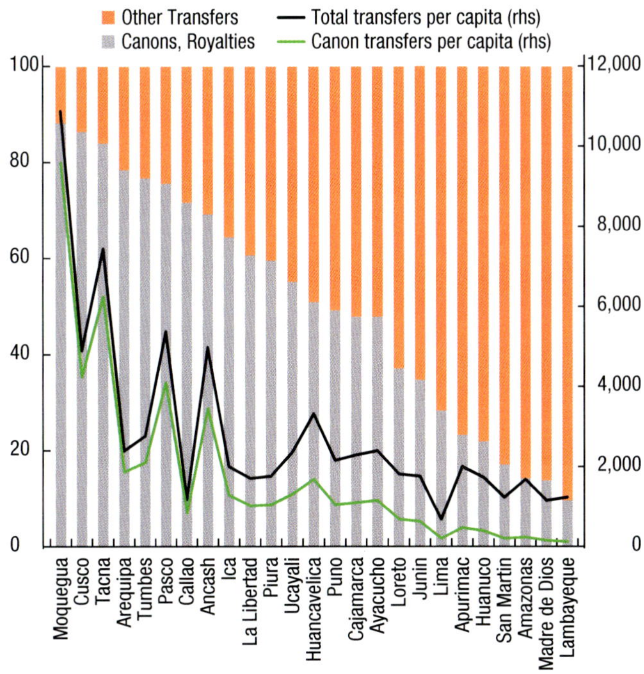

Sources: Peru's Ministry of Finance; and IMF staff calculations based on ENAHO.

household surveys. Similarly, the poverty rate fell from 13.8 to 8 percent,[17] with the rural sector registering the steepest improvement—a reduction in the poverty headcount of close to 15 percentage points.

In line with previous results (Yamada, Castro, and Baciagalupo 2012), household survey data shows that income of the poorest increased significantly faster than that of higher-income individuals during the boom (Table 8). While the population in the 1st to the 4th deciles saw their real income rise by more than 8 percent (annualized rate), individuals in the 10th decile experienced income growth of below 3 percent per year.

The labor income gains were broad-based at the sectoral level. Between 2007–11, real labor income per capita grew by an annualized rate of more than 10 percent in agriculture and fishing, as well as construction, and expanded at a still high rate of more than 5 percent per year in commerce and other services. In terms of employment shares, the manufacturing sector

[17]According to official reports, poverty in Peru fell by 14.6 percentage points during the same period. At least two methodological elements drive this difference. First, SEDLAC's poverty measure is based on monetary income, while official measure is based on consumption; second, poverty lines are different.

Table 8. Peru: Real Income per Capita Growth (2007–11)

Decile	Annualized Growth Rate
1	8.3%
2	8.9%
3	8.3%
4	8.2%
5	7.8%
6	7.5%
7	7.0%
8	6.0%
9	4.9%
10	2.7%

Source: IMF staff calculations based on World Bank SEDLAC data.

shrank while services, extraction, and mining activities and especially construction grew strongly (Figure 36).[18]

Looking at the breakdown by education shows that employment and income grew across education levels, albeit at varying speed (Figure 36). While the number of jobs rose strongest for higher education levels, real income per capita growth had the opposite pattern with the strongets growth for lower-skilled workers. Low-skilled workers' income grew at a steep pace (an annualized rate of about 11 percent) while income of skilled workers grew at half that rate. This shows the importance of supply factors—the number of skilled jobs grew strongly but income less so as the supply of skilled workers was expanding at the same time (Messina and Silva 2018).

Decomposing the Reduction in Inequality and Poverty in Peru

As in the case of Bolivia, we use Shapley decompositions to analyze how variations in the subcomponents of labor income and non-labor income affected inequality. We use information of a panel data version of the ENAHO (National Household Surveys of Peru) for the years between 2007 and 2011 to calculate income-based poverty and inequality indicators.

Changes in labor income explain about two-thirds of the reduction in inequality (Figure 37). While nonlabor income such as programs of public assistance or remittances played a role, they represent about 20 percent of the total reduction in the Gini coefficient. Similarly, evidence of the impact of changes in nonlabor income on poverty shows a negligible contribution.

[18]It is worth noting that although extractive sectors—mining and oil and gas extraction—pay the highest salaries in the country, they absorb a limited share of workers. About 2 percent of households have mining sector related income. In the case of oil and gas, that share is 10 times smaller, representing about 0.2 percent of total households. Agriculture and services—mainly wholesale and retail, have been the sectors employing most of the workers in Peru. More than 50 percent of households in the country had their labor income linked to one of these sectors between 2007 and 2011. While these two sectors have been central as employment generators, their workers are less well-paid on average.

Figure 36. Peru: Annualized Change in Real Labor Income per Capita Between 2007–11
(Percent)

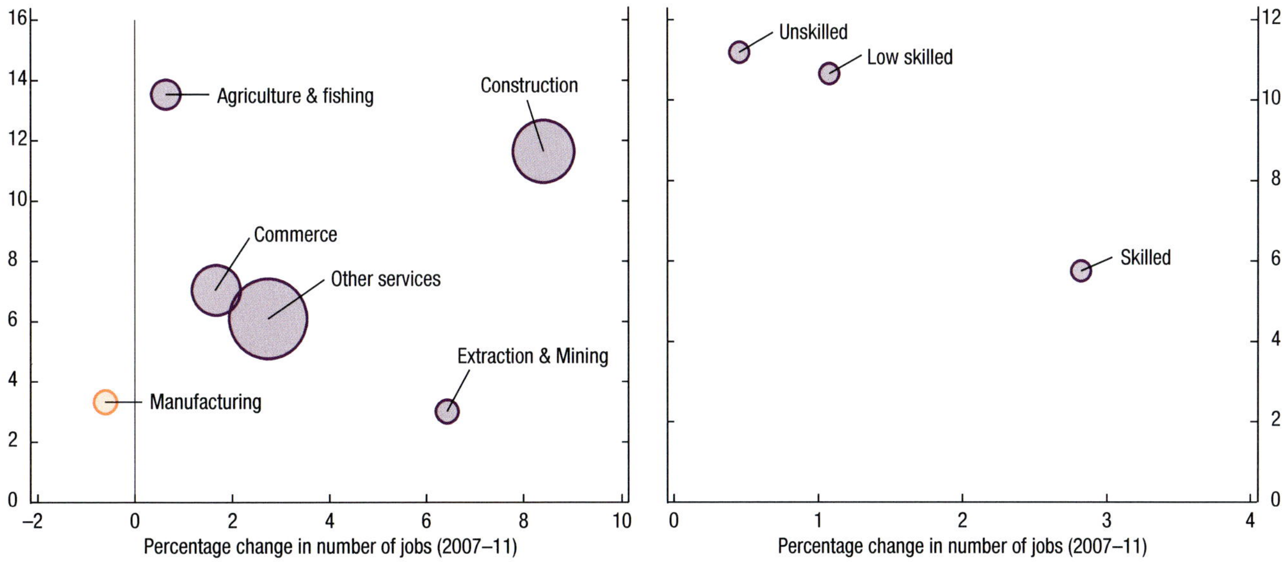

Source: IMF staff estimates based on Peru's Household Surveys (ENAHO).
Note: The size of the bubbles reflects the absolute change (between 2007 and 2011) in the number of individuals whose incomes depend on each of the sectors. In orange, a negative change.

Source: IMF staff estimates based on Peru's Household Surveys (ENAHO).
Note: Unskilled (never attended school or incomplete primary education); Low skilled (complete primary or incomplete secondary education); Skilled (complete secondary, incomplete tertiary or complete tertiary education).

Figure 37. Peru: Poverty and Inequality: Shapley Decomposition by Income
(Change between 2007–11)

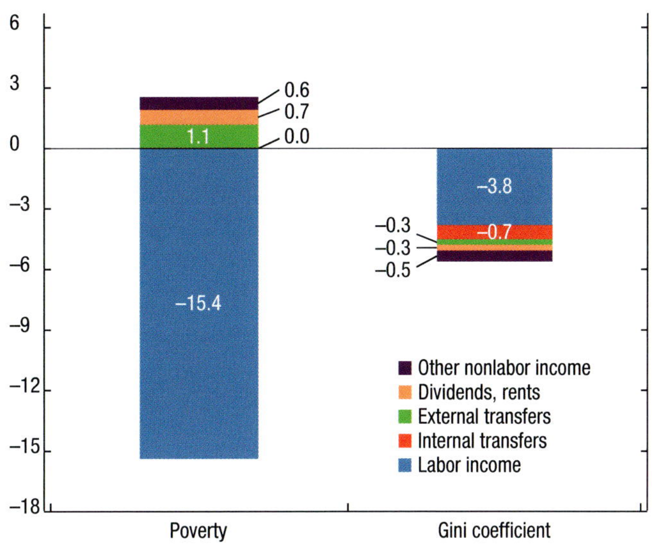

Source: IMF staff calculations based on Peru's Household Surveys.
Note: Poverty is calculated as the percent change. Gini coefficient change based on re-scaled Gini coefficients in the range (0–100).

Table 9. Peru: Composition of Households' Total Income

	2007	2008	2009	2010	2011
Labor	83.6	84.2	84.9	84.8	85.8
Nonlabor	16.4	15.8	15.1	15.2	14.2
Of which: Current Transfers[1]	*9.4*	*9.0*	*9.0*	*8.6*	*8.3*
Of which: Programa JUNTOS	*0.5*	*0.7*	*0.3*	*0.3*	*0.3*

Source: IMF staff calculations based on Peru's Household Surveys (ENAHO)

[1]This includes transfers from within the country: pensions, transfers from individuals and institutions, public and private.

Again, this is perhaps not surprising given that nonlabor income comprises less than 20 percent of total income (Table 9).

Our previous sections' results suggest that workers in two important sectors in terms of employment improved their labor income significantly–agriculture and services (representative of rural and urban sectors, respectively), thus improving inequality indices given their low-salary levels. In the case of poverty, most of the reduction was driven by improvements in urban areas, where employment in the services sector is dominant.

Changes in employment and salaries of workers with lower education levels (unskilled and low skilled) were one of the main factors behind the reductions in inequality and poverty (Figure 38). About 30–40 percent of the change in inequality and poverty was due to higher incomes of those groups (workers who attained incomplete secondary education or less). But skilled workers (those with at least secondary education) also played an important role due to the wide distribution of income for this group—while some households in this group are in the very highest income decile, many others were close to the poverty line.

The direct effect of an expansion of the extractive sector was an increase in inequality. As mentioned above, salaries in the extractive sector are among the highest in the country—further growth in wages in that sector thus increased inequality explaining the negative direct effect (Figure 39). But the indirect effect of an expansion in the extractive sector, including spillover effects to the nontradable sector (services sector) were a key driver of inequality reduction, in line with our previous case studies. Income associated with the services sector represents more than half of all sources of family income in Peru. Any growth in the services sector thus has immediate and large effects on poverty and inequality. Wholesale and retail constitute the largest subsector, generating the bulk of employment. Meanwhile, construction and hotels and restaurants were two sub-sectors that expanded particularly strongly during the commodity boom, both in terms of employment and salaries.

Figure 38. Peru: Poverty and Inequality: Shapley Decomposition by Skill Level
(Change between 2007–11)

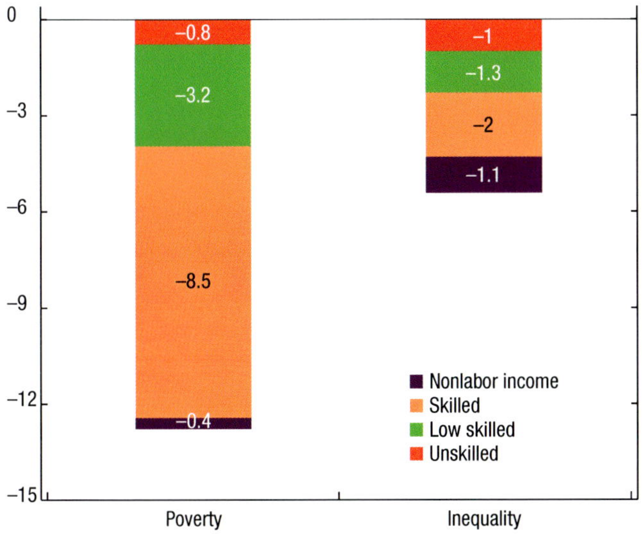

Source: IMF staff calculations based on Peru's Household Surveys (ENAHO).
Note: Poverty is calculated as the percent change. Gini coefficient change based on re-scaled Gini coefficients in the range (0–100). Unskilled (Never attended school or incomplete primary education); Low skilled (complete primary or incomplete secondary education); Skilled (complete secondary, incomplete tertiary or complete tertiary education).

Figure 39. Peru: Poverty and Inequality: Shapley Decomposition by Sector
(Change between 2007–11)

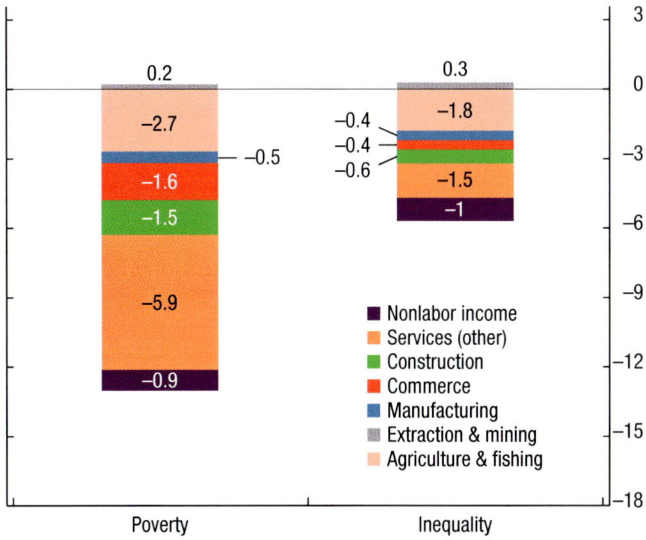

Source: IMF staff calculations based on Peru's Household Surveys (ENAHO).
Note: Poverty is calculated as the percent change. Gini coefficient change based on re-scaled Gini coefficients in the range (0–100).

The Impact of the Resource Boom at the Local Level

Empirical Strategy

To capture the impact of the resource boom on local income, employment, poverty, and inequality in a similar way to the Bolivia and Brazil case studies, we estimate the following equation (at departmental level rather than at the municipal level due to data constraints):[19]

$$\Delta y_{i,2011} = \alpha + \beta \Delta x_{i,2011} + \gamma \Delta y_{i,2007} + \delta y_{i,2007} + \rho Z_i + \epsilon_i$$

where $\Delta y_{i,2011}$ is the change in an income, employment, inequality or poverty indicator between 2007 and 2011 in department i and $\Delta x_{i,2011}$ is the change in the explanatory variable (real per capita canon transfers to departments). β will measure the effect of regional fiscal transfers on our set of income and

[19]The household survey data are not representative at the municipal level. Having to work at the departmental level significantly reduces he power of the regressions. Additionally, the period of analysis is somewhat shorter here than in the analogous analysis for Bolivia and Peru. The results here should thus be taken more as a high-level exposition.

Table 10. Peru: Impact of Canon Transfer on Select Indicators

	Poverty	Inequality	Income per Capita	Unemployment
Canon Transfers	−0.28***	0.07	0.35*	0.18

Source: IMF staff calculations.
Note: The table reports the standardized coefficients, indicating how many standard deviations the dependent variable will change, per standard deviation increase in the predictor variable.
$^*p < 0.10$; $^{**}p < 0.005$; $^{***}p < 0.01$.

employment related indicators. The level of the dependent variable in 2007 ($y_{i,2007}$) and its change between a previous round (2004 to 2007 – $\Delta y_{i,2007}$) were also included to capture convergence effects and department-specific trends. Additionally, we included a set of dummy variables of geographic controls Z_i. We are not able to discriminate between the fiscal channel and other channels given that the only data we have are on fiscal transfers.

Results

Table 10 shows the results from the above specification. They point to a significant reduction in poverty and an increase in per capita income in departments which experienced a larger growth in per capita natural resource transfers (and supposedly in natural resource production per capita). No significant effects on inequality and unemployment rates are found, on the other hand, at departmental level. The table shows standardized coefficients, indicating that increasing canon transfers by 1 standard deviation leads to a reduction in the poverty headcount of about 0.28 standard deviations and to an increase in income per capita of 0.35 standard deviations. These results match those for Brazil and Bolivia to some degree, by highlighting the reduction in poverty achieved in regions was directly impacted by the commodity boom. Note that we are not able to discriminate between fiscal or market-based channels here since the explanatory variable is canon transfers per capita, which capture both channels.

Last, as in the other countries studied above, there is some evidence that the consequences of large and concentrated resource rent sharing at the subnational level warrants close study in Peru. Figure 40 shows that canon transfers are strongly associated with total transfers, indicating that there is no other transfer which "offsets" large natural resource transfers. And Figure 41 then shows that regions with very high natural resource transfers suffer from absorptive capacity constraints, as illustrated by a strong negative correlation between budget execution and canon transfers per capita.

Figure 40. Canon per Capita and Total Transfers per Capita at the Regional Level in Peru
(Average 2009–17)

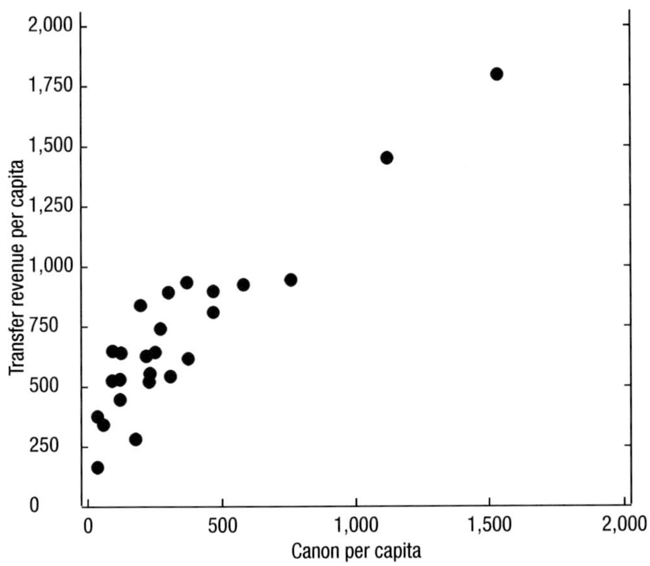

Source: IMF staff calculations based on Congreso de la Republica: Unidad Técnica "Observatorio de la Descentralización."

Figure 41. Canon per Capita Transfers and Budget Execution at the Regional Level in Peru
(Average 2009–17)

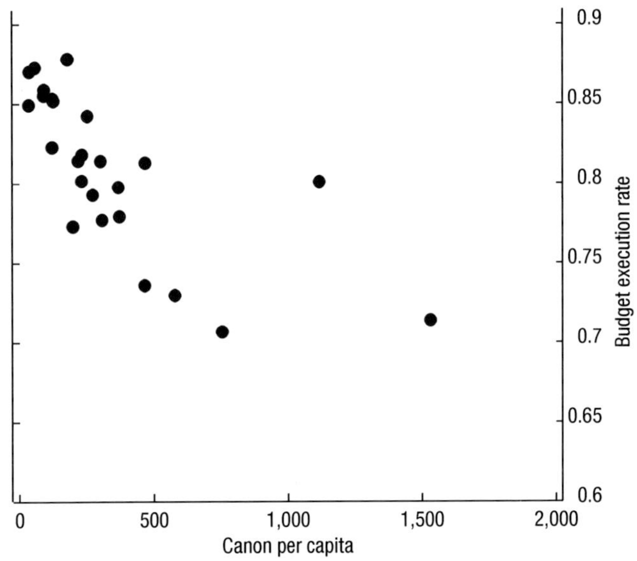

Source: IMF staff calculations based on Congreso de la Republica: Unidad Técnica "Observatorio de la Descentralización."

Takeaways

Several common themes emerge from our case studies. In all three countries, the lower deciles of the income distribution experienced large income gains during the boom, with income flat only for the top decile (see similarity with cross-country regression results in Table 2). We show that the extractive sector boom in the 2000s tended to reduce inequality and poverty—with the results stronger for the latter—both due to higher fiscal spending and increased labor demand in low-skilled sectors such as construction and services directly tied to the resource production. We also find that spillovers from the commodity sector to the nontradable sectors are at the core of labor income gains for low-skilled labor and the key driver for the observed poverty and inequality reductions. Overall, while we find that government transfers played a smaller role than labor income gains, this is likely to be different when looking only at the lowest income decile(s), as becomes clear from the literature studying Brazil. Box 3 at the end of the chapter, presents a brief overview of inequality developments in Mexico, which did not have a commodity boom, and shows that labor income inequality did not fall there.

At the local level (but not necessarily at the aggregate level), direct spillovers from the extractive sector to the nontradable sectors appear more important than the fiscal windfall. Mineral mining is more labor intensive than hydrocarbons production and mineral municipalities consequently experienced larger shifts in employment composition and reductions in poverty during the boom than oil and gas municipalities.[20]

Looking at local data can also shed light on the success of natural resource rent sharing with subnational governments which is now common in many countries. Previous evidence points towards the importance of improving governance and government capacity for the success of decentralization of fiscal windfalls. Caselli and Michaels (2013) for Brazil, Arrellano-Yanguas (2011) for Peru and Perry and Olivera (2009) for Colombia all find that there are serious governance and/or capacity constraints which hamper the use of fiscal windfalls at the subnational level. In line with these results, we show tentative evidence that the local fiscal windfalls might not always have had fully satisfying results, leading to large increases in public sector employment in oil and gas municipalities, for example, as well as issues with absorptive capacity. In Chapter 6, we will come back to this issue.

[20]Our work complements a growing literature that looks at the impact of natural resource extraction by using microdata and exploiting local variation. Aragon and Rud (2013) show that a large gold mine in Peru leads to positive spillovers to the local economy through its demand for inputs, while Loayza and Rigolini (2016) find that the presence of gold mines in Peru reduces local poverty but increases consumption inequality. For Brazil, Cavalcanti, Da Mata, and Toscani (2019) find that the direct market effect (abstracting from the fiscal channel) of having an oil sector is beneficial for municipalities and leads to structural transformation away from subsistence agriculture toward the services sector over the long-term. Benguria, Saffie, and Urzua (2018) corroborate these finding for Brazil over the recent boom period by showing a compression in the wage premium as well as significant employment gains in the commodity sector with some positive spillovers to the nontradable sectors, combined with employment losses in the tradable sector in regions affected by the positive commodity price shock. For Chile, Pellandra (2015) shows that the commodity boom in the 2000s significantly reduced poverty and inequality by increasing unskilled workers' wages and compressing the wage premiums. Alvarez Garcia, and S. Ilabaca (2017), also for Chile, come to a similar conclusion. Also see Cust and Poelhekke (2015) for an overview of the literature.

Box 3. Inequality Developments in a LAC Country without a ToT Boom: The Case of Mexico

Compared to other Latin American countries, Mexico did not experience a strong decline in inequality over the last decade. And in stark contrast to the commodity boom countries, labor income did not contribute at all in reducing inequality. Government transfers did support the reduction in inequality to some degree, but their role remains much smaller than in OECD countries. For further details see Lambert and Park (2019).

Inequality in Mexico only slightly declined over the last decade, while labor income inequality worsened. The Gini coefficient for total household income declined by about 5 percent during 2004–16. In contrast, labor inequality increased and the Gini coefficient for household labor income (wages and self-employment income) remains well above the Gini coefficient for total income.[1]

Labor income contributed to a small increase in inequality during 2004–16, which was more than offset by government transfers. A Shapley decomposition of the change in the Gini coefficient between 2004 and 2016 shows that government monetary transfers account for about 16 percent of the total reduction in inequality over that period. Public transfers also played a significant role in the reduction of poverty over the same period.

Figure 3.1. Gini Coefficient for Household Income

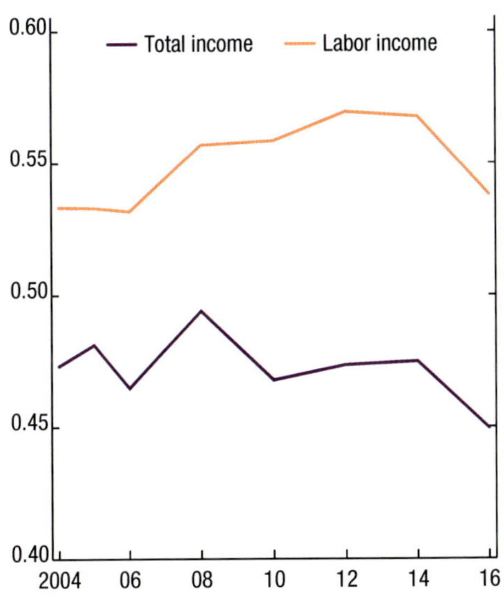

Sources: National Institute of Statistics and Geography (INEGI); and IMF staff calculations.

Mexico's social assistance programs cover households at the bottom of the income distribution well. 31 percent of the households in the bottom income quintile benefit from Mexico's conditional cash transfer program *Prospera* (formerly known as *Oportunidades* and initially launched as *Progresa*), which has served as a model for many countries around the world. Similarly, the share of households benefiting from old-age social assistance is three times higher in the first income quintile than in the fifth. *Prospera* and old-age social assistance programs account for about three-quarters of the decline in the Gini coefficient coming from government transfers, while they represent about half of the total government transfer amount received by an average household.

[1]Calculations based on Mexico's national survey on household income and expenditures (ENIGH).

Box 3. Inequality Developments in a LAC Country without a ToT Boom: The Case of Mexico *(continued)*

Figure 3.2. Shapley Decomposition of the Change in the Gini Coefficient for Total Household Income
(Between 2004–16)

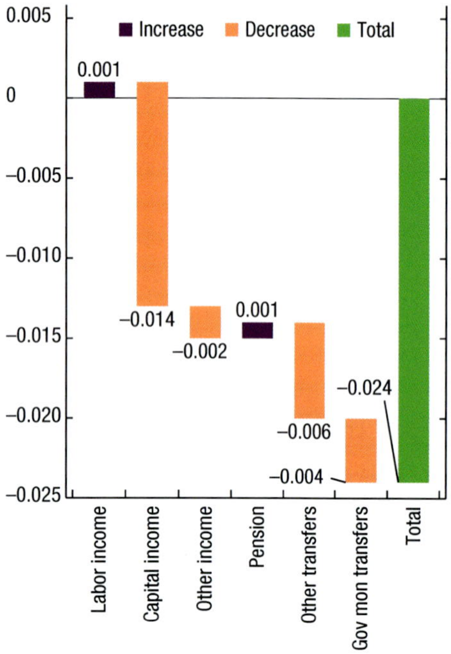

Sources: National Institute of Statistics and Geography (INEGI) and IMF staff calculations.

Figure 3.3. Coverage of Government Transfer Programs by Household Income Quintile, 2016

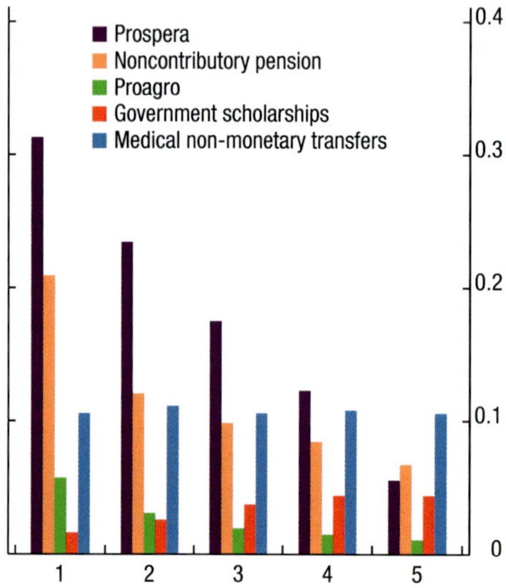

Sources: National Institute of Statistics and Geography (INEGI); and IMF staff calculations.
Note: Coverage is computed at the household level.

CHAPTER

4 Model-Based Case Studies: Bolivia and Paraguay

Motivation

We now turn to a model-based assessment of the impact of the commodity boom in Bolivia and Paraguay to complement the previous empirical evidence. We define commodities broadly in this section, to include both extractive industries (oil and gas but not minerals for the purposes of the model) and the agricultural sector. The model allows us to trace out and quantify the channels by which agricultural and energy commodity price shocks affected inequality, poverty, and growth during the 2000s. They also allow us to see the impact of various tax and spending policies.

As previously discussed, Bolivia is a highly commodity dependent economy. Paraguay too, is strongly commodity dependent but with a much larger share of agricultural commodities, relative to Bolivia's dependence on extractive industries (Figure 42). This difference in the *type* of commodities produced will allow for interesting variation which we can exploit.

Model

To trace out the links between the commodity boom and inequality reduction in Bolivia and Paraguay, we use a dynamic general equilibrium model that has a continuum of heterogeneous households, including farmers; informal, private and public sector workers; and entrepreneurs. The model is calibrated to the pre-boom period using macroeconomic and household survey data for Bolivia and Paraguay, and then the price shocks, structural changes (migration and skill changes) and policy changes are fed into the model to test its predictions for the boom period to calculate a new steady state. We discuss the analysis of the boom phase in this chapter and come back to the bust phase and its policy implications in Chapter 5.

Figure 42. Commodity Exports[1]
(Percent of GDP)

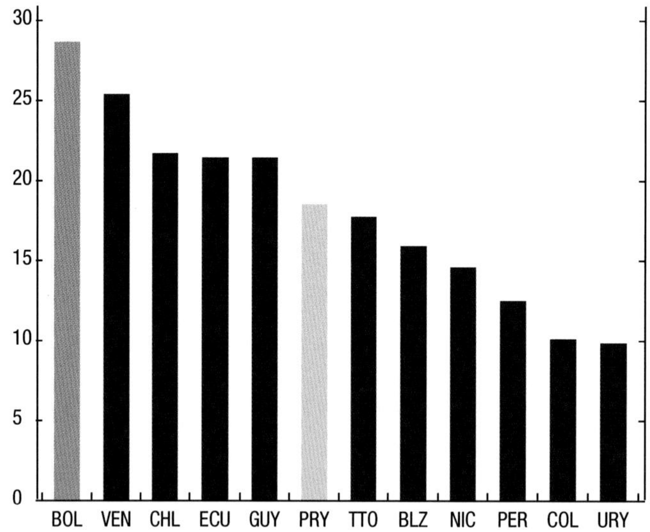

Sources: UN Comtrade; Gruss (2014); IMF, *World Economic Outlook*; and IMF staff calculations.
Note: Country list uses International Organization for Standardization (ISO) country codes.
[1]Average ratios to GDP for 2010–12. Excludes precious metals and re-exports. Venezuela data refer to net oil exports.

A sketch of the model can be found in Box 4 with further details in Appendix 1.

The principal features include:

- Significant roles for the agricultural and energy sectors, with exports heavily concentrated in these sectors.
- A relatively small manufacturing sector.
- A relatively large public sector, and small industrial sector.
- A relatively basic financial sector, with limited opportunities for risk sharing.

In view of the dominance of the energy sector in the Bolivian economy (less so in Paraguay), its key features are explicitly considered in the analysis. The sector comprises large enterprises whose productive technology is intensive in capital while its share of employment relatively small, so direct benefits are highly concentrated. The price of energy (mainly oil and gas products) is determined on international markets, and it is sold on both domestic and international markets. The firms in the oil and gas sector pay taxes and royalties to the government, which are one of the main sources of government revenue.

The model also reflects the overall productive structure of the economy as well as sectoral interlinkages. Agriculture supply is built from the bottom up, and it comprises the output from a large number of households ranging from subsistence farms (that barely generate any surplus) to higher productivity farms active in domestic and international markets. Fluctuations in agricultural prices play an important redistributive role in the model as higher prices distribute income toward surplus-producing farmers. The industrial sector is composed of firms that produce manufacturing goods and services using capital, labor and energy as inputs. Urban households, which range from high-skilled and very productive households, to low-skill and low-productivity households, supply their labor to the industrial sector or to the government, or are self-employed in household enterprises (the informal sector). As in the case of agricultural prices, prices of services also have an important redistributive role as most of the low-skilled and low productivity households are concentrated in the informal sector of the economy.

The model captures the key role of government. Investment expenditure on infrastructure acts as a growth engine that increases total factor productivity of the private sector. Social spending has a critical role in promoting inclusive growth and reducing poverty. The public sector constitutes one of the most important categories of employment and has a significant impact on the incomes of a large share of urban households. Subsidies and price controls affect the domestic price of energy. On the revenue side, the government collects taxes and royalties from energy sector enterprises and various taxes from other agents in the economy.

Calibration of the Pre-Boom

Parameters and initial values of the variables are chosen so that the model accurately reflects the averages of key economic indicators in the pre-boom period (2000–05) for Bolivia and Paraguay.

Table 11 reports the main features of the two economies in the initial steady state (average 2000–05), before simulating a commodity boom. The two economies differ in some key characteristics that will be important in explaining the results of the simulations for the commodity boom. Agriculture has a larger share in Paraguay (22 percent) and energy plays a bigger role in Bolivia (this is even more striking if we exclude the hydropower energy production

Table 11. Initial Steady State for Bolivia and Paraguay

	Bolivia		Paraguay		
	Data	Model	Data*	Data	Model
Shares in GDP					
Agriculture	15.9	16.3	27.1	15.9	27.0
Energy	12.9	12.6	2.0	12.9	2.0
Manufacturing	18.2	18.7	16.1	18.2	16.0
Services	53.1	52.5	54.8	53.1	55.0
Export	30.0	28.6	32.3	50.4	25.2
Commodity export	22.6	19.9	13.0	22.6	23.0
Government revenue	21.8	24.6	15.3	15.3	14.2
Royalties	4.7	4.5	3.1	3.1	1.9
Informal sector (% of workers)	74.2	65.5	72.2	72.2	48.5
Households (% of total)					
Entrepreneurs	na	5.0		na	5.0
Rural	37.5	37.5		43.7	43.7
High skilled	37.3	37.3		36.2	36.2
Income Gini					
National	61.0	62.7		54.3	52.6
Rural	62.0	65.0		56.0	56.9
Urban	55.0	55.1		51.0	51.0
GDP by Expenditures					
Private consumption	73.7	71.9		61.6	59.5
Public consumption	11.9	12.0		9.5	9.5
Food consumption (% of total consumption)	39.0	39.1		33.0	31.8
Private investment	8.9	9.8		10.2	10.2
Public investment	5.5	6.3		6.0	20.9

Source: IMF staff calculations.
Note: Average: 2000–05
*For Paraguay, it excludes the production and export of hydro power from the Binational Damns.

in Paraguay given the special nature of the latter).[1] These differences are reflected in the different commodities exported by the two countries: energy and agricultural products for Bolivia and agricultural products for Paraguay. In turn, these commodity exporting sectors are characterized by different technologies and types of labor employed. Hence, a commodity boom would affect economic households' income differently in Bolivia and Paraguay because of these key differences.

While the services sector represents a large share of the economy in both countries, there are striking differences in terms of the composition. In Bolivia, financial services are important while in Paraguay most services are commercial activities related to border-town trade and therefore employ mostly low-skilled workers. The large share of agriculture and services in both economies is also reflected in pervasive informality.

[1]For the purpose of studying commodity cycles, the production and export of hydroelectric sector (by the so called Binationals) in Paraguay should be stripped out. While energy produced in Paraguay and then exported to Brazil and Argentina is a large share of GDP, prices are administered by international treaties and do not follow international price trends. Hence, they are not subject to commodity prices cycles that are the focus of this study. If we exclude the Binationals production from GDP, then the share of energy drops to 2 from close to 15 percent in Paraguay.

The sectoral data are matched by calibrating the differences in total factor productivity (TFP) across sectors in the economy, as well as the sector-specific parameters of the production functions, and implicit tax rates.[2]

The model also replicates key distributional features of household-income data for Bolivia and Paraguay. The persistence and variance of the households' idiosyncratic shocks are calibrated to reproduce the Gini coefficients observed in the data.[3] In addition, the model is calibrated to match households' consumption patterns with the objective of capturing the distributional implications of the policy changes.

Then the price shocks, structural changes (migration and skill changes) and policy changes are fed into the model to test its predictions for the boom period and forecast the impact of the commodity bust.

Bolivia

Replicating the Boom

In Bolivia, during 2006–14, agricultural commodity prices (mainly soy) increased by more than 60 percent, while natural gas prices (its most important commodity export), increased by nearly 75 percent, relative to levels during 2000–05 (Figure 43). At the same time, GDP growth doubled, and the Gini coefficient fell by nearly 9 Gini points (see Chapter 3 for additional details).

To simulate the commodity price boom, we depart from the calibrated pre-boom steady state and compute a new steady state associated with higher commodity and energy prices as well as other changes (which are taken as exogenously given in the model) that took place during the commodity boom period. These are:

1. Improvements in the fraction of skilled workers, which went from 38 percent in the pre-boom period to 47 percent in the boom period.
2. Observed changes in the rural/urban composition of the population, which went from 38 percent in the pre-boom period to 31 percent.
3. The following changes in policies:

[2]The trade balance is set to zero. This implies that the trade numbers (for example, for exports) can deviate from what is seen in the data, especially in the case of Paraguay where the average trade balance has been significantly different from zero.

[3]*For Bolivia,* the official household survey is MECOVI. For Paraguay, the households survey is the Encuesta Permanente de Hogares (EPH), conducted by Dirección General de Estadística, Encuestas y Censos.

Figure 43. Bolivia GDP Growth and Commodity Prices
(Percent)

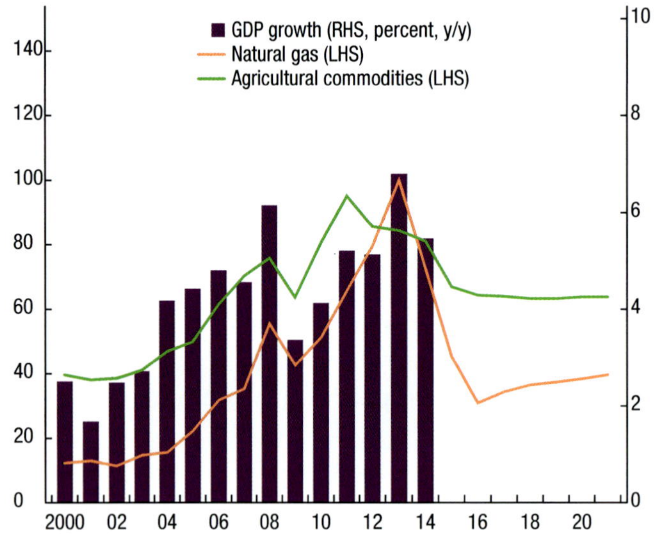

Sources: National Statistics Agency (INE); and IMF staff calculations.
Note: y/y = year over year.

- o Increases in cash transfers expenditure: these expenditures went from being 0 to approximately 2 percent of GDP in the boom period.
- o Price controls: average inflation of Bolivia for the boom period was under 3 percent per year, despite increases of 300 percent in international energy prices and nearly 100 percent in international agricultural commodities. In line with the information regarding the use of price controls to energy and food items during the period, we restrict the domestic price of energy and the food in the model to go only up to 10 percent during the boom period.
- o Higher government wages: the government wage bill as share of GDP went from being 8.8 percent in the pre-boom period to 9.5 percent during the boom.
- o Higher revenue mobilization: total government revenues went from about 22 percent of GDP in the pre-boom period to close to 30 percent of GDP in the boom period. To match this information, effective tax rates in the model increase so that the model matches the revenue sources by tax instrument observed in the data.

Sector TFPs are set so that sector shares for the new steady state match the data. However, to illustrate the impact of individual shocks, TFP is kept at the levels of the pre-boom steady state. Otherwise, TFP could vary across

Figure 44. Model Simulations of the Commodity Price Boom in Bolivia, Change in Growth, 2006–13
(Percentage points)

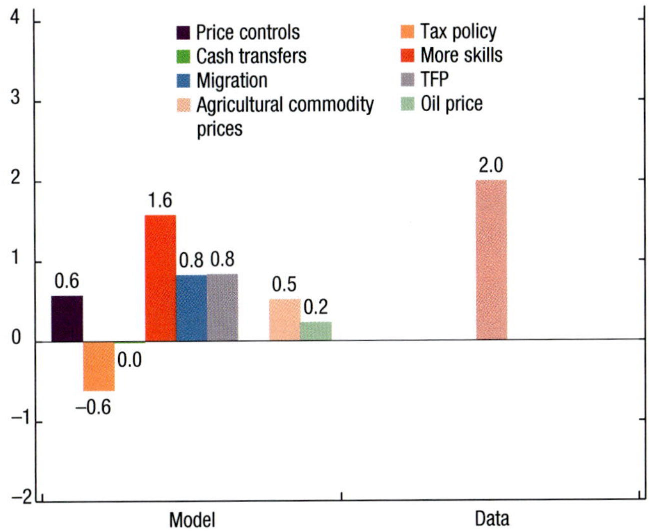

Source: IMF staff calculations.
Note: TFP = total factor productivity.

the new steady states associated with each individual shock, complicating the comparison of the impact of each shock.

Results

Impact on Transitional Growth

Although the balanced growth path in the steady state does not change (that is, the slope of the GDP path does not pivot), the various shocks can increase/decrease the level of GDP (that is, shift the GDP path) between two steady states. The necessary growth to reach those new levels of GDP could be thought of as *transitional growth* (that is, an increase/decrease in the rate of growth relative to the balanced growth path).

The 2 percent higher growth observed during the period 2006–14, relative to pre-boom years (2000–05, considered the initial steady state) is explained by a combination of factors (Figure 44). Higher agricultural prices (we simulate a positive shock of 60 percent) have a larger direct impact than higher energy prices (we simulate a positive shock of 240 percent to match the increase in the average price of WTI between the two periods), but this is unlikely when we consider indirect effects, something we look at in detail below. The largest impact on growth comes from the substantial increase in the fraction of skilled individuals in the urban labor force. This helped the industrial sector to expand and take advantage of the increased private sector productivity. Migration also played an important role. Indeed, the share of the rural population fell by nearly 7 percentage points during the boom.[4] As workers in the urban sector tend to be more productive, this helps boost growth. Some of the fiscal policies undertaken included higher taxes, which taken in isolation had a moderate negative impact on growth. Increased revenue, for example, from royalties, was spent on additional cash transfers and infrastructure. The latter, indirect channel also contributed to increasing growth as higher investment boosted TFP.

Higher Energy versus Higher Agricultural Prices

Despite the lower magnitude, the agricultural price shock has a stronger direct effect on growth relative to the energy shock for two main reasons. First, labor intensity is higher in the agricultural sector than in the oil/gas sector (where it is zero in the model). Hence, increasing incomes of agricultural households has a larger impact on aggregate demand than increasing incomes of households that benefit directly from oil (which in this case are the entrepreneurs whose share in the total population is only 5 percent). Second, the agricultural sector is larger than the energy sector as a share of GDP.

In addition, higher energy prices generate opposing forces. First, higher energy prices increase the value of the marginal product of capital in the energy sector. This higher profitability increases the incomes of the entrepreneur, pushing consumption, and investment up. Higher aggregate demand from the households engaged in the energy sector results in second round effects because this higher demand for goods increases the prices of nontradable goods, stimulating the nontradable sector of the economy. Second, higher energy prices exert a negative influence on growth in some sectors of the economy. In particular, capital intensive sectors (which are also energy intensive, since capital and labor are complementary) must pay higher costs for their inputs. However, controls to energy prices reduce the negative impact on production costs of the modern sectors of the economy (manufacturing and services) relative to what would happen if the price was allowed to pass through fully. Third, higher international prices of energy generate an important indirect effect via higher government revenues, which allow higher investment in productive infrastructure that increases private sector productivity. The overall impact on output is significantly positive.

[4]Note that migration is exogenous in the model but might well have been (partly) driven by the commodity sector as the expanding services sector in urban areas demanded more labor.

Figure 45. Model Simulations of the Commodity Price Boom in Bolivia, 2006–13

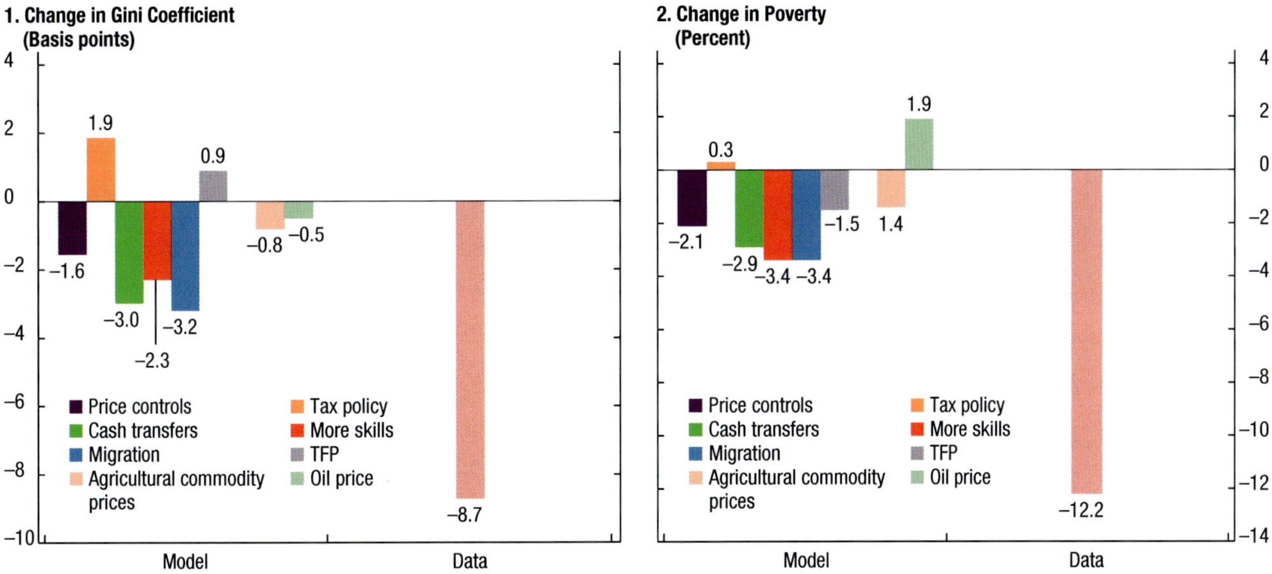

Source: IMF staff calculations.
Note: TFP = total factor productivity.

Impact on Inequality

Higher prices for tradable agricultural commodities increased the demand for the corresponding raw agricultural products (which are processed minimally and then exported), ultimately raising the prices of agricultural goods, and the incomes of rural areas (Figure 45, panel 1). The result is higher incomes for farmers in rural areas relative to urban households. In addition, higher agricultural goods prices (that is, food) do have a negative impact on urban households' budgets, although this effect is mitigated in the case of Bolivia by the food price controls. In addition, higher incomes boost demand for non-tradable goods, which bids up wages for the lowest skilled workers (including those in the informal sector). While this has the result of lowering the aggregate Gini, the fact that nontradable services are located mostly in urban areas partially offsets this by increasing urban-rural inequality. This is one reason why the impact of the increase in agricultural commodity prices on the Gini is milder than the reduction of poverty, as shown in Figure 45, panel 2. Poverty is simply measured by the percent of households below the poverty line in the whole nation, no matter in which area they live. Indeed, agricultural price increases generates a significant decline in poverty, despite its relatively small share of GDP.[5] Energy prices are found to have a lower direct impact

[5]Another reason for the smaller effect than in the case of Paraguay is that there is a bigger share of smaller farmers in Paraguay than Bolivia. Smaller farmers are more likely to be poor and hence benefit from the positive agricultural commodity price shock.

on inequality (as the gas sector has a very low labor intensity) and a negative impact on the poverty rate. But they have an important indirect effect via higher government revenues, allowing for a substantial expansion in social programs. This accounts for an important share of the observed decline in inequality and poverty.[6]

The increase in average skill level of the workforce (the share of workers with education higher than high school rose from 30 percent to 45 percent between 2000 and 2012) led to higher incomes in urban areas. This also made skilled workers less scarce, which ultimately reduced the skills wage premium, and led to a sizable decline in inequality and poverty. Migration leads to the biggest reduction in inequality and poverty at the same time, given much lower incomes of poor farmers relative to urban workers, notwithstanding a wide dispersion in incomes of the latter group. Other government policies, such as the tax increase, and the increase in TFP resulting from infrastructure spending led to an increase in inequality. The increase in TFP leads to increased inequality as the sector which benefits the most is the manufacturing sector (where the TFP increased by 14.7 percent).[7] This adds to inter-sectoral income inequality, making urban areas more prosperous in comparison to rural areas.

Paraguay

Basic Facts During the Boom

In the period 2006–13, Paraguay benefitted from agricultural and livestock commodity prices increasing by about 60–70 percent. During the same period, the country performed robustly, growing at about 5 percent a year, above peers in the region both in terms of output and income per capita growth. Coincidentally, despite inequality remaining elevated (a Gini coefficient of 0.50), poverty and income inequality declined, signaling that growth was inclusive.

Data for Paraguay show that during 2006–13 employment grew relatively more in rural areas, where the agriculture and livestock sectors are more prominent, and for low-skilled workers (Figure 46). Salaries also show that incomes increased relatively more for lower-skilled labor (Figure 47). However, during the same period Paraguay experienced other structural changes that could have affected income distribution, including polices. The share of population living in urban areas grew by 2 percentage points, as a result of

[6]Indeed, cash transfers have a much bigger impact on inequality than growth in the model.

[7]To be consistent with the sectorial composition of the economy in the second steady-state the TFP of manufacturing had to increase by 14.7 percent (all other TFP remained at their levels in the steady-state).

Figure 46. Paraguay: Employment by Area
(Percent of population age 25–64)

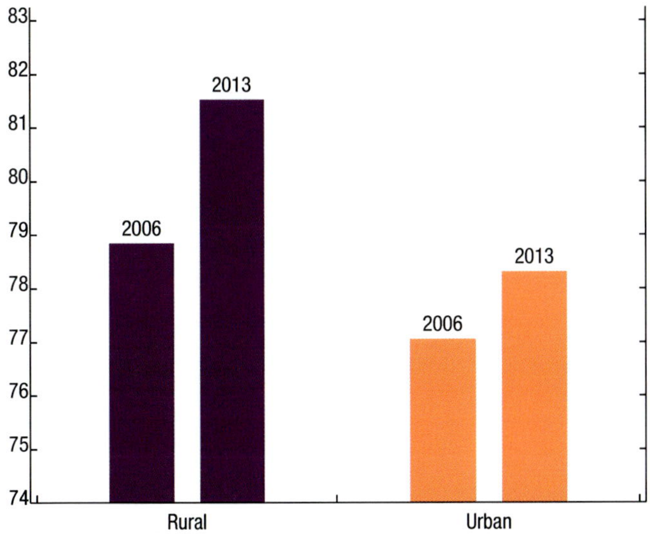

Source: SEDLAC (CEDLAS and the World Bank).

Figure 47. Paraguay: Wages Primary Versus High-Skilled Sectors
(Ratio primary to high skilled services)

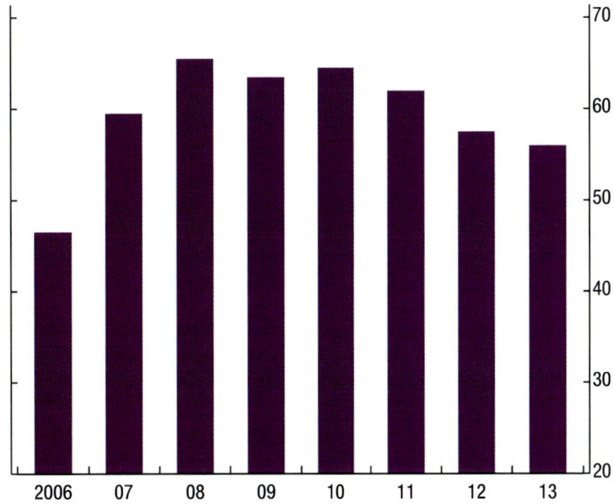

Source: SEDLAC (CEDLAS and the World Bank).

migration from rural areas. This might have helped with equalizing incomes between rural and urban centers. In addition, skills among the labor force exogenously increased, supporting a reduction of the skill premium.[8]

Government policies were also important. In 2004, a VAT reform extended the tax base even to basic goods (though at a lower rate) increasing the revenue from indirect taxes by 2 percent of GDP. Transfer programs also increased but remained relatively small (below one-half of GDP). The government expanded and hired significantly more workers, whose salaries are generally higher than other sectors, with only some exclusions. Finally, the government stepped up in-kind transfers, such as health care in mid-2000s, which grew by 2 percentage points of GDP in the period 2006–13. Health care spending increased in both new public care providers and assisted medical treatments, including new subsidized medicines.

These changes, along with the increase in agricultural commodity prices (includes a price increase of both agricultural goods such as soy, and meat-related products) are used to compute a new steady state associated with the commodity boom.

[8]The share of urban workers with low skills fell by more than 10 percentage points to slightly more than 50 percent.

Figure 48. Model Simulations of the Commodity Price Boom in Paraguay, Change in Growth, 2006–13
(Percentage points)

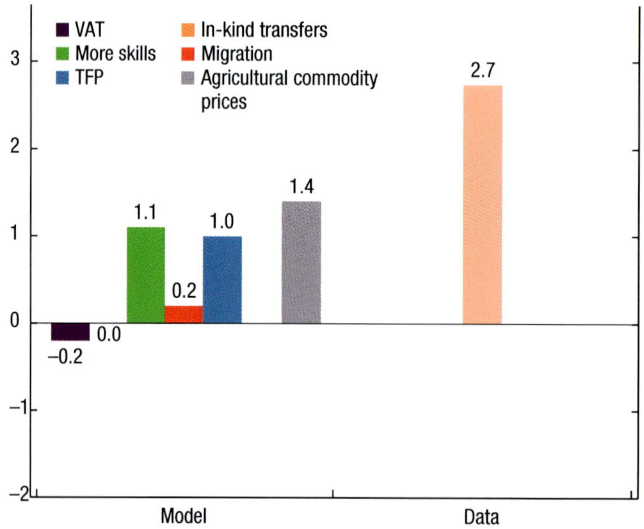

Source: IMF staff calculations.
Note: TFP = total factor productivity.

Results

Impact on Transitional Growth

Figure 48 displays the result of the simulations of an agricultural commodity price increase of 60 percent, along with the other macroeconomic developments highlighted in the previous section. During the commodity boom, growth averaged 4.7 percent, a marked increase from about 2 percent in the pre-boom period. In other words, the transitional growth rate increased by 2.7 percentage points in the period 2006–13. Model results suggest that the commodity boom might have accounted for nearly half of the increase, a much larger role than the one played in Bolivia by a similar shock as the agricultural sector in Paraguay is larger and more productive. The rise in average skills of the workforce accounted for the other half of it. Migration had some positive impact on growth as workers moved from less-productive rural jobs (you can think of self-sufficient agriculture) to higher-productivity sectors in urban centers. But the impact is much less than in the case of Bolivia for two main reasons. First, migration in Bolivia was a much larger phenomenon (the rural population decreased by 7 percentage points as opposed to just below 2 percentage points in Paraguay). Second, since the agricultural sector is more productive in Paraguay, the gains in terms of performance from the migration to the urban more productive sectors is smaller. Increases in TFP, mostly

Figure 49. Model Simulations of the Commodity Price Boom in Paraguay, 2006–13

1. Change in Gini Index (Basis points)

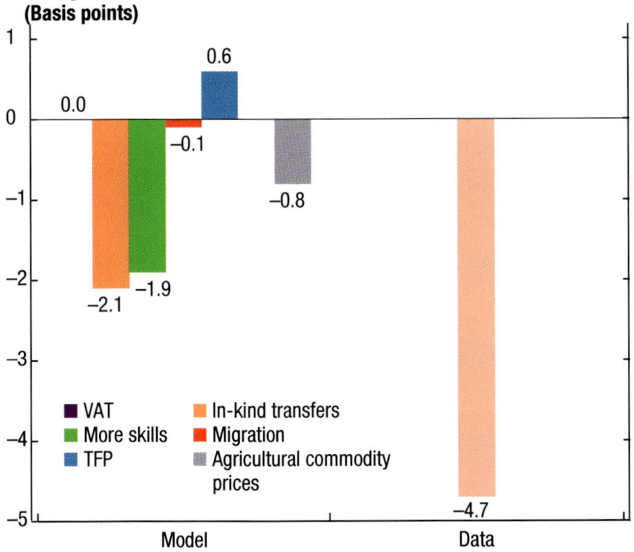

2. Change in Poverty (Percent)

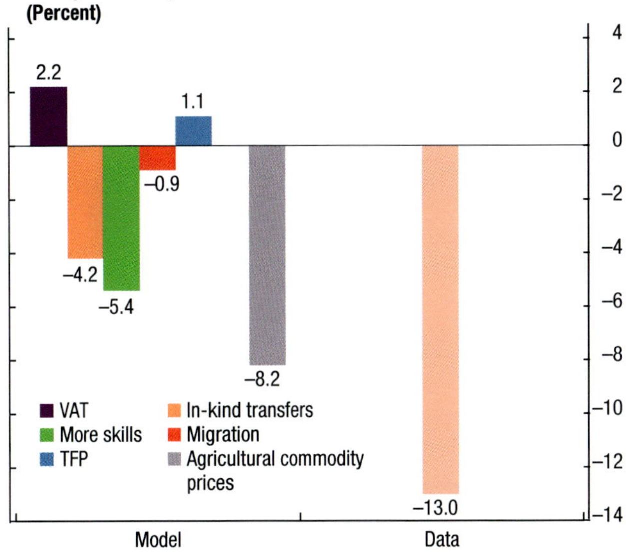

Source: IMF staff calculations.
Note: TFP = total factor productivity.

in the manufacturing and services sectors, had also a significant impact on growth. Policies such as the increase of VAT base had a negative impact on growth, albeit small, given that it discouraged consumption.

Impact on Inequality

Figure 49 displays the results of the same simulation on indicators of income inequality. The model suggests that growth arising from the boom in agricultural commodity prices was also conducive to reducing inequality, accounting for a significant share of the reduction in the Gini coefficient between 2006–13 (about 20 percent of the fall or about 1 Gini points) and to an overwhelming reduction in poverty, explaining more than half of the fall in the percentage of households below the poverty line. This was the result of two forces: (1) an increase in rural relative to urban incomes; and (2) a rise in the number of low-skilled jobs and incomes, including in the nontradable sectors, similar to the case of Bolivia. The decrease in the Gini coefficient is muted given land is extremely concentrated in Paraguay (the land Gini is 93.0).[9] A larger supply of skills in the labor force (more skills) was the cause of equalizing forces between high skilled and low skilled wages (reduction of

[9]If, for example, we decreased the concentration of land to a Gini of 78.0 in the rural sector, the impact of the increase in agricultural prices is higher and accounts for about 40 percent of the actual change of the Gini.

skill premium). This was the other largest channel through which inequality fell after 2005.

The impact of migration on inequality is driven by forces different than in the case of Bolivia. As already mentioned, migration flows were relatively small in Paraguay. In addition, the migration toward urban sectors not much more productive than agriculture did not create a big gain in terms of labor incomes. Lastly, by moving to urban centers more households pay VAT, which is regressive and has a negative impact on lower-income workers.

The increase in TFP affected more urban sectors and supported income in those areas relative to the rural ones, increasing intersectoral inequality. The increase of indirect taxes (VAT) had the potential to increase inequality by a large magnitude. However, given that most of the rural informal sector does not pay VAT, the actual impact is much less. VAT affected poverty negatively, mostly in urban centers. The large increase in health care spending had the effect of reducing inequality, although its impact was mitigated given that health care centers are still concentrated in urban areas.[10] Combining all the policies, the increase in health care dominates the negative impact of the VAT reform on measures of income inequality and the net impact is a reduction of the Gini index by about 1.5 basis points.

Key Takeaways and Differences between Bolivia and Paraguay

The dynamic general equilibrium model exploited in this chapter for studying the case of Bolivia and Paraguay demonstrates how commodity price shocks can affect both GDP and inequality in the case of commodity exporters. It also underscores, however, that the impact depends on the importance of the sector affected in each country, the type of commodity and its production technology, and government policies.

The type of commodity shocks and the commodity sectors' technology matter. Both agricultural and energy price shocks increase potential GDP. However, regarding inequality, positive agricultural price shocks appear to have a larger *direct* effect on inequality reduction given the relatively high labor intensity (in particular, low-skilled) of the agricultural sector and the low-income level of the majority of the population living in rural relative to

[10]As a caveat, we do not dispose of data on the distribution of health care as in-kind transfers by income percentiles so we make some assumptions. We assume that the increase in health care spending provided by the central government (Ministry of Health) (most of the increase, 1.7 percent of GDP) would benefit disproportionally low-income categories while the increase observed at the *Instituto de Prevision Social* (IPS) (0.3 percent of GDP) benefitted the relatively better-off. The geographical distribution of health care center also affected the distribution of the transfer between urban and rural population, with a two third of the centers located in urban cities.

urban areas. Demand pressures on the nontradable sector also appear to be an *indirect* effect of the price shock, as income increases are more diffused and demand for auxiliary services also grows. Both developments within the agricultural sector and the pull effect on the nontradable sectors generate an increase in wages and incomes in rural areas relative to urban areas and an increased demand for low skilled relative to high skilled jobs at the national level. This reduces the skill premium.

Positive energy price shocks, however, have the potential *direct* effect of increasing income inequality as they employ relatively more skilled labor and the technology is more capital intensive. However, as shown in the case of Bolivia, an increase in energy prices and revenue from royalties seems to have a larger *indirect* effect, including ultimately increasing the demand for auxiliary and other nontradable sectors. This can more than offset the direct effect, especially in the presence of administered energy domestic prices, and when those resources are spent on social transfers or infrastructure. Cases of commodity-exporting countries such as Congo, however, where higher tax revenues were not spent efficiently for new social programs, show how the direct effect can dominate and lead to income inequality rising, although poverty did fall significantly (IMF 2014b).

The size of the commodity sector also matters. For example, the agricultural commodity price shock was of a similar magnitude in Bolivia and Paraguay but had a much bigger impact on growth and inequality in the latter. This is consistent with the agricultural sector being larger in Paraguay.

Finally, policies can also make a big difference. Some policies can pose trade-offs between the impact on growth and inequality. Cash transfers, price controls and some tax policies (that improve the progressivity of the system) can have a mild or even negative impact on growth but can help improve income distribution. In the model simulation, for the same energy price shock, the impact on inequality can vary depending on the policies enacted, for example price controls or cash transfers. Bolivia displayed the largest inequality fall in the region during the commodity boom, as increased cash transfers and price controls played key roles. These policies complemented the impact of not only the commodity price shocks but also the significant migration and increased education levels. Finally, while infrastructure spending may have a large positive impact on growth it generates a trade-off in terms of income inequality if the improvements favor urban relative to rural areas.

Box 4. General Structure of the DGE Model

- Small open economy with five consumption goods: domestic food, imported food, manufacturing, services, and energy.
- There are several types of households: (1) rural and urban, (2) private sector and government employees, (3) entrepreneurs (capital holders), and (4) low-skilled and high-skilled workers. There is a continuum of households, equal ex ante, but facing uninsurable idiosyncratic risk. Households solve dynamic optimization problems taking prices and government policies as given.
- There are five sectors, each characterized by different technologies: (1) agriculture (with rural households, employing land and low-skilled labor); (2) manufacturing (with a technology using low-skilled labor and capital, owned by entrepreneurs); (3) services (produced either by urban households in family businesses, with low-skilled labor; or by entrepreneurs in the industrial sector, with high skilled labor); and (4) energy (with a technology exploiting high-skilled labor and capital, owned by entrepreneurs). Finally, entrepreneurs also export agricultural goods.
- The only financial assets available are one-period bonds, and they are traded among households to allow for risk sharing. The interest rate on these bonds, the wage for public and private employees, the price of domestic food, and the price of services are determined by supply and demand forces in equilibrium.
- The government collects tax revenue (on income, consumption, etc.) and royalties. This revenue is used to finance investment in infrastructure that increases private sector productivity and other government expenditures (including public sector wages, energy subsidies and pro-poor spending).
- The model is thus a dynamic general equilibrium including a continuum of households facing idiosyncratic risk (as in Aiyagari 1994, Nishiyama and Smetters 2005, 2007) and also multiple sectors (as in Greenwood, Hercowitz, and Krusell (1997), Gollin, Parente, and Rogerson (2006), Restuccia, Dennis, and Zhu (2008) and Herrendorf, Herrington. and Velentinyi (2015) the structural transformation literature).

Chapter

5 Explaining Post-Boom Developments

What Do the Findings About the Boom Suggest About the Post-Boom Phase?

Essentially, the post-boom phase is a negative wealth shock that propagates through the economy via the various channels discussed in previous chapters but in the opposite direction. At a first pass, and assuming policies do not adjust, based on the work in Chapters 3 and 4, lower commodity prices will thus reduce potential GDP and medium-term growth for commodity producers, and hence adversely affect poverty through opposite forces to those at play during the boom.

For inequality, as in the boom phase, the net impact is not so clear cut. For example, in the case of Bolivia, the model of chapter 4 suggests that the net impact on inequality depends on what happens to income in urban relative to rural areas. The decline in agricultural prices reduces rural incomes and increases rural poverty. At the same time, the decline in energy prices was much steeper than for agricultural prices. Hence incomes in urban areas could potentially fall faster than in rural areas, reducing intersectoral inequality and, potentially, the actual Gini coefficient. To this direct effect, we also need to add indirect effects via demand for nontradable goods, which as in the boom period could potentially more than offset the direct effect of energy prices on inequality.

Several further considerations apply. First, it is important to note that while the channels by which commodity prices affected inequality and poverty during the boom will also be present in reverse during the post-boom period, they need not be symmetric. For example, many commodity exporters saw significant migration to urban areas from rural areas. This may not reverse in the post-boom period given high costs associated with moving. If it does reverse, however, this would exacerbate rural-urban inequities and increase the overall impact on inequality. Another important channel is the fiscal one. Any fiscal revenue loss associated with lower commodity prices could have a significant impact on social safety net and infrastructure spending. Of course, some countries used the commodity windfall to structurally improve their fiscal buffers, offering the fiscal space to offset lower fiscal revenues associated with lower terms of trade for an extended period of time. We will return to this issue in the following.

The type of commodity also matters, with regions exposed to metal price declines as opposed to hydrocarbons price corrections likely facing larger direct employment losses (for similar movements in prices) given the relative labor intensity of both sectors, while agricultural price declines would have a sizable impact on poverty given how close rural incomes are typically to the poverty line. But given that the largest price corrections occurred for hydrocarbons, it is not ex ante clear which type of commodity exporter should be most affected.

In summary, it seems clear that in general lower commodity prices should lead to a decline in potential growth and the pace of poverty reduction in commodity producers, whereas the impact on inequality is much less clear cut given the various forces at play.

How Did Actual Developments Compare to These Predictions?

As discussed in Chapter 1, poverty stopped falling in commodity exporters in 2014–19 and in some cases even reversed some of the previous gains. Inequality on average kept falling albeit at a slower pace.

On average, as a reaction to the adverse shock commodity exporters protected expenditures even as revenues fell, leading to rising fiscal deficits and increasing debt (Figures 50 to 53). Counter-cyclical fiscal policy might thus have played an important role in explaining why social gains did not revert as much as might have been expected in commodity exporters.

However, given the permanent nature of the shock, excessive accommodation, especially in countries with no fiscal space or fiscal space at risk, carries important risks for medium-term poverty reduction. As an illustration, consider Colombia and Ecuador, which suffered negative terms of trade shocks of a similar magnitude (Figure 54). The two countries also had similar trends in poverty prior to the commodity shock (Figure 55). Ecuador's fiscal deficit increased by 3.7 percentage points of GDP in 2013, already placing it on a divergent fiscal path relative to Colombia.

Figure 50. Overall Balance
(Percent of GDP)

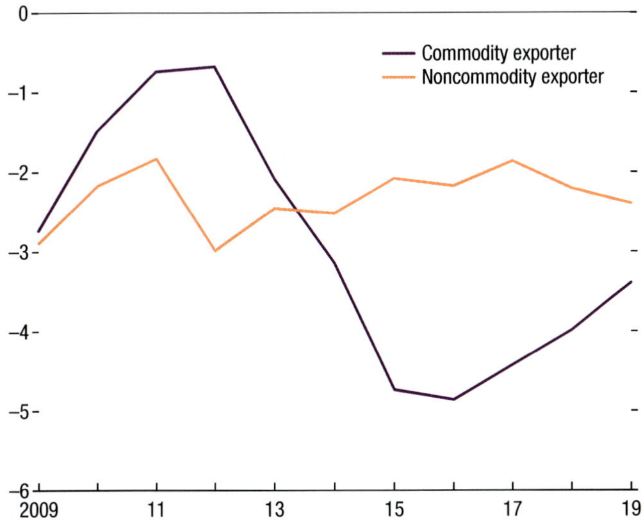

Sources: IMF, *World Economic Outlook database*; and IMF staff calculations.

Figure 51. Government Debt
(Percent of GDP)

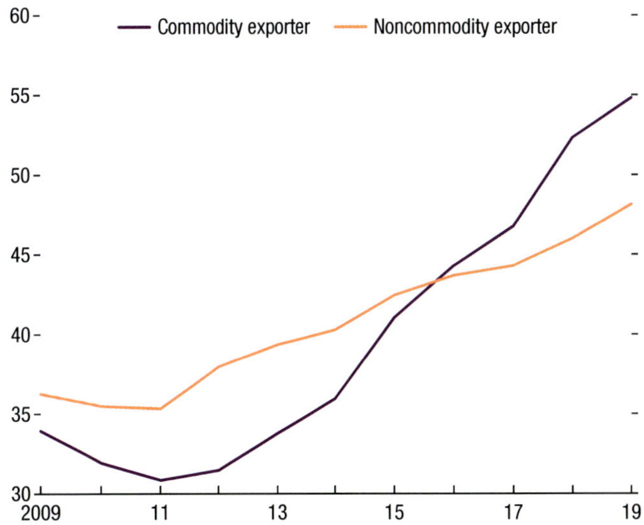

Sources: IMF, *World Economic Outlook database*; and IMF staff calculations.

Figure 52. Revenues
(Percent of GDP)

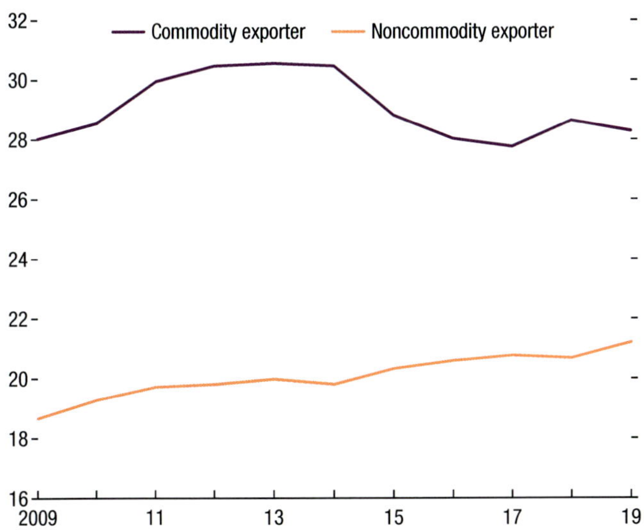

Sources: IMF, *World Economic Outlook database*; and IMF staff calculations.

Figure 53. Expenditures
(Percent of GDP)

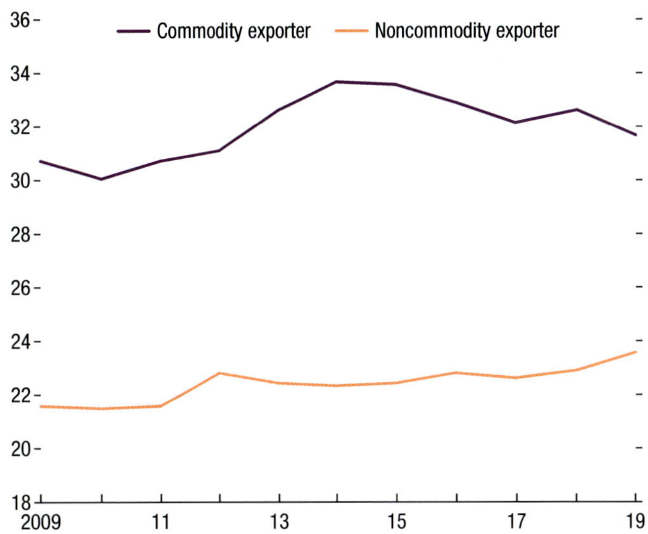

Sources: IMF, *World Economic Outlook database*; and IMF staff calculations.

Figure 54. Commodity Terms of Trade and Fiscal Deficit in Colombia and Ecuador
(Percent)

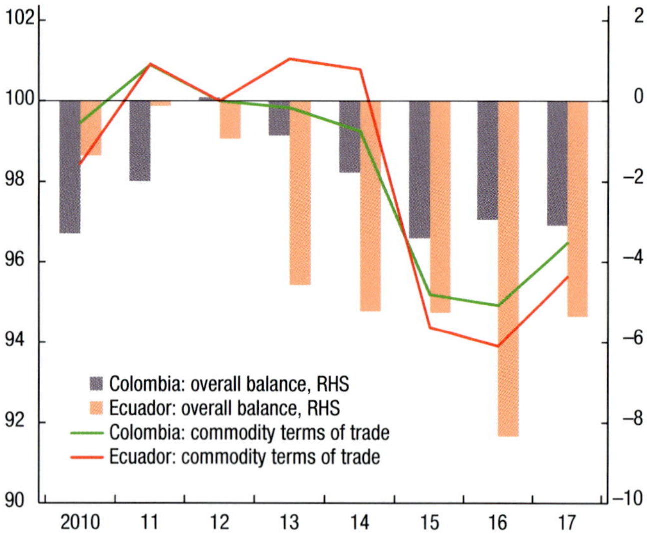

Sources: IMF, *World Economic Outlook database*; Gruss and Kebhaj (2019); and IMF staff calculations.

Figure 55. Poverty Rate in Colombia and Ecuador
(Percent)

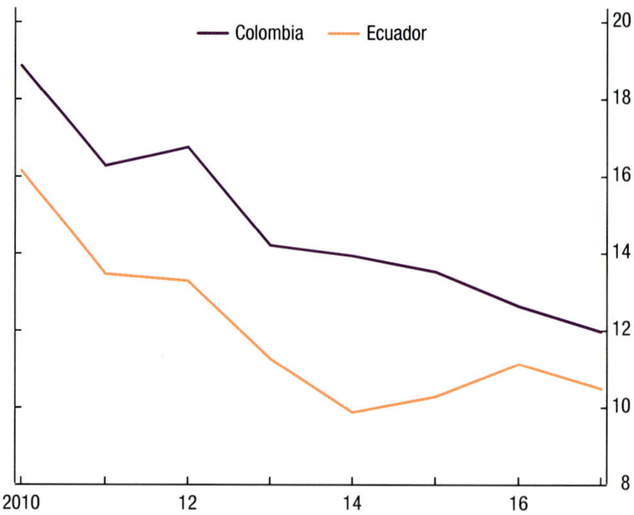

Source: Inter-American Development Bank, SIMS database.

When the oil price shock materialized in 2014/15, guided by its fiscal rule, Colombia reacted by providing some fiscal accommodation by letting the fiscal deficit widen to somewhat above 3 percent of GDP from a low base. Ecuador provided similar accommodation in terms of the change in the fiscal deficit. However, considering its higher starting point, Ecuador's fiscal deficit reached 8 percent of GDP in 2016. In 2017, the authorities began a multi-year effort to reduce the fiscal deficit, and put debt on a downward trajectory, thereby increasing Ecuador's resilience to future commodity shocks. Poverty continued to fall in Colombia post-2014, while it increased in Ecuador over 2014–16 (Figure 55). This highlights the importance of building buffers during the boom times and to smoothly adjust to permanent shocks.

As discussed in more detail in Box 5, Peru provides a good example of both. During periods of particularly high commodity prices, Peru ran important budget surpluses, building buffers for an eventual reversal (Figure 56). After the commodity terms of trade had peaked in 2011, this allowed the country to provide fiscal accommodation, supporting further poverty reduction, without endangering sustainability. Bolivia adopted a similarly prudent stance during the commodity boom but reacted with more aggressive fiscal loosening after the shock.

Figure 56. Peru: Commodity Terms of Trade and Fiscal Balance
(Index and Percent of GDP)

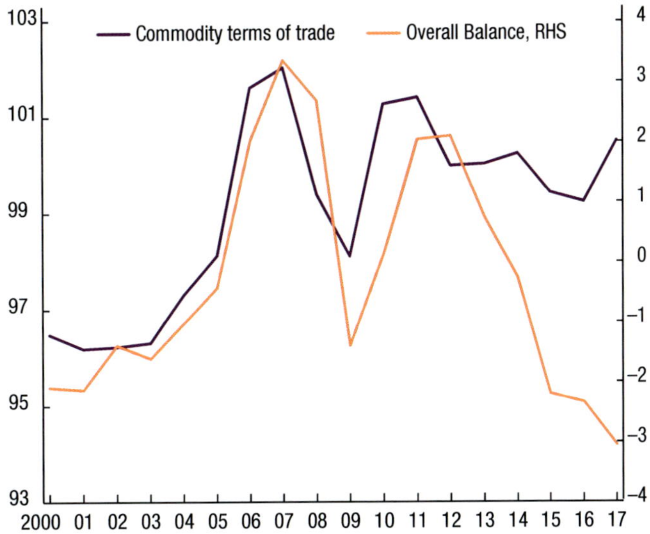

Sources: IMF, *World Economic Outlook database*; and IMF staff calculations.

Box 5. Peru: Inequality and Poverty after the Commodity Boom

Figure 5.1. Annualized Percent Change in Real Labor Income per Capita, 2011–15

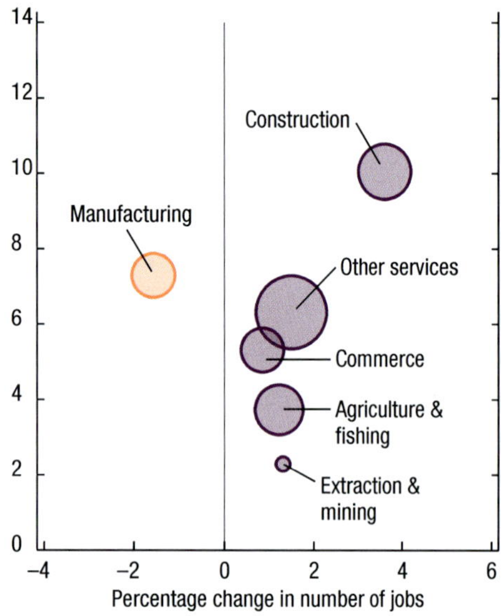

Sources: Peru's household surveys (ENAHO); and IMF staff calculations.
Note: The size of the bubble corresponds to the absolute change between 2011 and 2015 in the number of workers in each sector whose income depend on each of the sectors. In orange, a negative change.

Peru's export prices reached a peak in 2011, and between that year and 2015 they fell by 27 percent, mostly driven by metal and oil prices. The economy continued growing at high and positive rates (4.8 GDP annual average growth rate between 2011–15), just not as high as the peak of the boom (6.7 percent growth rate between 2007–11). In line with the new external conditions, the strong growth rates observed in real income and employment in previous years also moderated.

Notwithstanding lower commodity prices, Peru continued to reduce poverty and inequality during the post-boom period, but at a much slower pace. The remarkable changes in both indicators between 2007–11, with reductions of about 13 and 5.5 percentage points, respectively, were cut by nearly two-thirds during the post-boom period.

Compared to the results described in Chapter 3, variations in nonlabor income gained in relative importance when explaining the reduction in both indicators. The manufacturing sector, one of the weakest performers during the post-boom period in terms of number of jobs, contributed negatively to poverty reduction. Regarding educational levels, the most vulnerable (that is, low-skilled and unskilled workers) did not contribute as much as in previous years to poverty reduction.

Box 5. Peru: Inequality and Poverty after the Commodity Boom *(continued)*

Figure 5.2. Decompositions of Poverty and Inequality Changes by Employment Sector, 2011–15
(Percent)

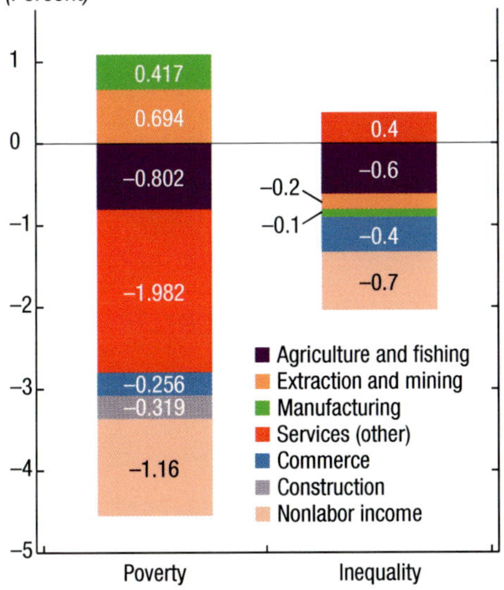

Sources: Peru's Household Surveys (ENAHO); and IMF staff calculations.

Figure 5.3. Decompositions of Poverty and Inequality Changes by Worker Skill Level, 2011–15
(Percent)

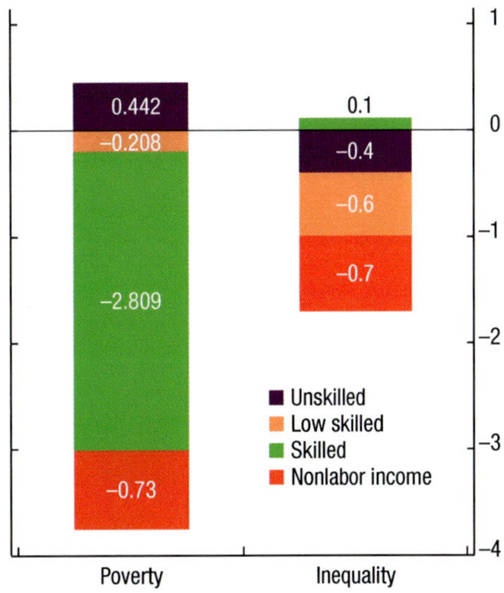

Sources: Peru's Household Surveys (ENAHO); and IMF staff calculations.

Chapter

6 Policies to Tackle Poverty and Inequality: Where to Next and What Needs to Be Done?

Short-Term Policy Priorities Following the COVID-19 Shock

As discussed in chapter 1, the COVID-19 shock is leading to unprecedented job losses and hardship. It is exactly the nontradable low-skilled service sector jobs—which helped to lift many out of poverty and reduce inequality during the boom—that have been hit the hardest by the COVID-19 shock (WHD, REO October 2020). In some sense, the dynamics during the boom might have created a vulnerability for the COVID and post-COVID area. Many fear it will turn back the clock on years of social progress.[1] And experience from previous pandemics does not allay such concerns given pandemics typically lead to disproportionate jobs losses for individuals with basic education (versus those with advanced education) and an increase in inequality.[2]

Governments across the region have reacted with immediate and substantial policy responses to the COVID-19 shock. A description of these policies can be found at https://www.imf.org/en/Topics/imf-and-covid19/Policy-Responses-to-COVID-19, while IMF notes summarizing some of the key principles and considerations with regard to these policies can be found at https://www.imf.org/en/Publications/SPROLLs/covid19-special-notes.

While some progress has already been made during this crisis, cyclical policy priorities to help deal with such pernicious effects will likely include further expanding access to sick leave, unemployment benefits, and health benefits, especially for poorer segments of society who lack a savings cushion and often are not eligible for such benefits because they work in the informal sector, are self-employed, or are on temporary contracts. Introducing new transfers, boosting public work programs to offer job opportunities, giving financing

[1]https://www.ft.com/content/9be51e4f-e89f-4ffc-a6a7-1313240e0624

[2]https://blogs.imf.org/2020/05/11/how-pandemics-leave-the-poor-even-farther-behind/

opportunities to sustain employment, and progressive tax measures to avoid excessive deficits—all are likely to be part of the policy mix to take the edge off the devastating distributional consequences from the pandemic.

In the rest of this section, we look beyond the immediate crisis response to structural issues which were important prior to the shock and have likely become even more critical now. We focus on the role that can be played by central government fiscal policy, the allocation of revenue capacity and spending responsibilities at different levels of government, and other policies associated with labor markets, education, and diversification.

The Road Ahead: Structural Policy Discussion

Central Government Fiscal Policy

It is well established that Latin American tax and transfer systems are substantially less progressive than such systems in Organisation for Economic Co-operation and Development countries (Lustig 2012; Hanni, Martner, and Podesta 2015; OECD 2018). Lustig (2012) finds that in some Latin American countries, the net income of the poor and near-poor can be lower than it was before taxes and cash transfers. In-kind transfers in education and health, however, are progressive throughout the region.

Figure 57 illustrates this point in more detail. Fiscal policy is estimated to reduce income inequality by an average of about 15 percent across Latin American countries, with the majority of the reduction coming from spending on health and education, rather than traditional fiscal instruments such as taxes and transfers. More specifically, fiscal instruments with a direct impact on income reduce inequality by only 4 percent, compared to 8 percent in other emerging and developing countries and 35 percent in advanced economies. Looking specifically at personal income taxes, Hanni, Martner, and Podesta (2015) find that while maximum legal personal income tax rates in Latin America range from 25 to 40 percent, the effective tax rates tend to be substantially lower, with the effective rate for the top decile only at 5.4 percent on average. Exemptions, allowances, simplified regimes and evasion and avoidance all contribute to low effective rates (ECLAC 2019). Consequently, the redistributive impact of personal income taxes in Latin America is very limited, achieving a reduction of just 2 percent in income inequality, which contrasts markedly with the countries of the European Union, whose distribution improves more than 12 percent after income taxes (OECD 2018).

But progressive spending on health and education, especially in countries such as Argentina and Costa Rica reduce inequality by an average of 10 percent across LA. Fiscal instruments with an indirect impact on income (such

Figure 57. Effect of Fiscal Tools on Inequality
(Percent change in Gini Index)

Sources: Prepared based on data from Lustig (2018).
Note: Country list uses International Organization for Standardization (ISO) country codes. LAC = Latin America and the Caribbean.

as indirect taxes and tax exemptions) on average do not impact inequality in LA. To protect social progress, especially in countries with limited fiscal buffers which need to consolidate, there are several avenues central governments could take.

On the revenue side, IMF (2014a) recommends progressive personal income taxes as an important tool to achieve fiscal redistribution. Given the low effective rates of PITs in LA, revenues from personal income taxes could be increased. The effort should be focused on scaling back tax exemptions, avoiding preferential treatments and combating tax evasion and avoidance to increase the effective progressivity of taxes. A decrease in thresholds to bring more high-income individuals into the tax net can also be considered in some cases. Indirect taxes are already relatively high in Latin America and tend to be less progressive than direct taxes and thus in general might not be the ideal tool to raise revenues at this point.

On the spending side, given their regressive nature, universal price subsidies (for example, energy subsidies) could be further reduced even though they are already at relatively low levels in Latin America when compared to other emerging regions. Increasing the efficiency of spending could also play a role. For example, existing social transfers could be better targeted in many countries by making further use of means testing where feasible (IMF 2014a). Last, it is important to carefully calibrate whether and how to use the fiscal space generated by reduced interest rate expenditure following a primary balance adjustment. An overall package that combines both infrastructure spending and social transfers would likely be desirable in terms of ensuring beneficial growth and social effects over the medium term. Many Latin American countries have highly rigid current expenditure envelopes (for example Brazil and Colombia) which in the medium-term would benefit from reforms which allow for a higher share of capital expenditure.

Pension Reform

Pension systems play an important role for social outcomes, both directly and indirectly, given their central role in the social contract, the often-substantial redistribution between individuals and generations they entail, and their fiscal costs. Pension design is a hugely complicated task which aims to guarantee adequate pensions to the broadest possible part of the population in a fiscally sustainable way. As Figliuoli and others (2018) point out, in Latin America many defined benefit systems appear to face fiscal sustainability concerns given aging populations while defined contribution systems are struggling to produce socially acceptable replacement rates.[3]

Given its complexities, the issue of pension design is much beyond the scope of this paper. Moreover, the variety of pension systems in existence across Latin America means that any reform suggestion will have to be carefully calibrated to country-specific circumstance. Nevertheless, there are two issues with direct implications for poverty and inequality which come out of a thorough review of pension systems in the region by Altamirano and others (2018) that are worth discussing here:

1. Many Latin American pension systems have a long-minimum contribution period for an affiliate to become eligible for a pension (usually specified in terms of numbers of weeks or months of contributions). This

[3]Brazil had the defined benefit system with the largest sustainability concerns but pension reform in late 2019 substantially improved the fiscal outlook.

introduces a strong discontinuity, whereby replacement rates are low (or even 0 in the case of the defined benefit system in Peru) when a worker contributes for less than the minimum period but jump up to fairly generous levels (at least in many defined benefit systems) when he or she crosses that threshold. Given high informality in Latin America, especially among lower-income workers, many affiliates struggle to meet the minimum contribution period.[4] The minimum contribution period thus often ends up being highly regressive with lower-income workers de facto being taxed to pay pension subsidies to higher-income workers.

2. On the other hand, minimum pensions and non-contributory pensions tend to act as progressive tools in Latin American pension systems. Minimum pensions guarantee a pre-specified minimum pension amount to those workers who reach the requirements to retire. They thus tend to lead to higher replacement rates for lower-income retirees relative to higher-income ones. But minimum pensions still exclude those who do not meet the requirements to retire from the contributory pillars. To provide a safety net to this part of the population, non-contributory pensions can be a powerful tool when they are well-integrated with the overall system.

The afore-mentioned observations lead to important policy considerations: fixing the excessive generosity of certain defined benefit systems and addressing the large differences in eligibility for pensions are among the most important factors to reduce inequities (Altamirano and others 2018). And to protect the most vulnerable against old-age poverty, well designed minimum pensions and noncontributory pension pillars can be an important tool (see, among others, World Bank (2008)).

Colombia and Peru Case Studies

To provide a more concrete discussion of the role of pension reform in reducing inequality and poverty, we consider the cases of Colombia and Peru, two countries for which the IMF has recently published recommendations on pension reform. Both countries have a defined contribution and a defined benefit pillar which operate in parallel and de facto compete for affiliates. Both countries also have a relatively recent non-contributory program aimed at the elderly.

[4]Labor informality is often explicitly defined as work without social security contributions. In high-informality countries, many workers move between formal and informal sector jobs, leading to interrupted pension contribution careers. Freudenberg and Toscani (2019) show that in the case of Peru, workers on average contribute for 4–5 months out of a possible 12 months per year over their working life. This is similar to the level observed in the private sector in Mexico (IMF 2018c) and somewhat below the average in Chile (Benavides and Valdés, 2018).

In the case of Colombia, only about one-third of the pension-age population receive a contributory pension and about one-half of pension-age population is below the poverty line. Low coverage is in part a reflection of widespread labor informality and the relatively high contribution threshold for eligibility (1,350 weeks). For the few eligible, the replacement rate in the defined benefit pillar is relatively generous (70–100 percent) and benefits mostly the rich with about half of the implicit subsidy (difference between contributions and pension benefits received) being received by the top income quintile.

IMF (2018b) recommends that beyond parametric reforms (changing the retirement age and lowering the replacement rate in the defined benefit pillar), deeper structural reforms should aim to expand pension coverage while ensuring progressivity and fiscal sustainability. These include strengthening the non-contributory pillar, lowering the relatively high eligibility threshold (number of weeks), and guaranteeing a minimum pension.

In the case of Peru, high labor informality means that only about 30 percent of the economically active population are contributing to statutory pension schemes and less than 10 percent of workers in the bottom income-quintile do. Freudenberg and Toscani (2019) use affiliate-level information to project the replacement rate distribution and find that average replacement rates are likely to be low, at about 30 percent in both the defined benefit and defined contribution pillar.

The average masks substantial differences and inequities. In the defined benefit pillar, average replacement rates for those who reach the 20-year minimum contribution period, and who are thus eligible for a pension, are relatively high at roughly 60 percent. But about 60 percent of all affiliates are unlikely to reach the 20-year threshold, leading to a replacement rate of zero. Given that affiliates from the bottom income quintile are three times less likely to reach the threshold than affiliates form the top quintile, this implies highly regressive redistribution.

Large, albeit less pronounced, differences in replacement rates between groups of affiliates also exist in the defined contribution pillar. Affiliates with full contribution careers, generally high-income workers, are expected to have replacement rates about 40 percent even in one of our more conservative scenarios. On the other hand, workers with below average contribution densities (generally low-income workers) will have replacement rates substantially below 20 percent.

Several avenues for reform exist in Peru. Shortening the minimum contribution period from 20 to 15 years would allow more people to obtain a pension and thus raise the average replacement rate at a relatively limited fiscal cost (we estimate a gross cost of 0.05 percent of GDP). In the SPP (Peruvian private pension system using the Spanish acronym), broadening the contribution base or increasing contribution rates would have an important impact on replacement rates to guarantee adequate pensions, but could adversely affect labor formalization. Peru's current old-age transfer (Pension65) has been shown to have an important effect in reducing old-age poverty and could be strengthened and developed into a full-fledged non-contributory pension. As in Colombia, in the medium-term, a larger reform to restructure the system and avoid competition between the private and public pension plans should also be a priority.

Fiscal Decentralization

As discussed in Chapter 3, Bolivia, Brazil, and Peru all redistribute large parts of the fiscal windfalls from natural resource extraction back to subnational producer regions and local governments. Colombia also redistributes royalties to subnationals. A reform in 2012 substantially reduced the focus on producer regions, but a subsequent reform in 2019 partially reversed this to increase incentives for production (see Box 6 for further details, including on the frameworks in advanced economies such as Canada and Norway). As also underscored in Chapter 2, there is evidence of large increases in public employment and issues with absorptive capacity in some commodity-producing regions during the boom period. And since the end of the boom, the most important commodity-producing regions in Bolivia and Brazil, Tarija and Rio de Janeiro, respectively, have suffered severe fiscal sustainability problems. Does this presage the need for major reforms to decentralization frameworks?

As shown in Chapter 3, fiscal windfalls do have beneficial effects for producer regions. The case studies and previous work in the literature do also suggest, however, that highly concentrated and volatile resource transfers to subnational governments do not come without downsides. Indeed, sharing large amounts of natural resource revenues with subnational producers has several conceptual drawbacks. First, it is not clear whether geographical and geological differences between regions should determine fiscal envelopes given the large horizontal inequities this implies. Second, the volatile nature of natural resource revenues calls for careful intertemporal planning, which is even harder to achieve at the local level than at the national level. Third, resource revenues are essentially transfer revenues from a local government's perspective and thus do nothing to encourage accountability and the building of own-revenue bases. Fourth, when the fiscal windfall is large in per capita terms, it can lead to problems with absorptive capacity as well as governance (IMF 2009). Of course, the environmental impact of mining activity needs to be considered and creates a case for an additional transfer to producing regions.

More generally, it is also useful to think about how the distribution of natural resource rents among subnational units fits within the broader design of fiscal decentralization frameworks. At a conceptual level, fiscal decentralization frameworks can be assessed in terms of their *vertical gap, vertical balance, horizontal gap* and *horizontal balance* (Boadway and Eyraud 2018). The vertical gap refers to the shortfall in subnational own revenues relative to subnational spending, vertical balance refers to whether central governments transfers to subnational governments are adequate to fill the vertical gap such that subnationals can fulfill their spending responsibilities. While the vertical gap refers to the aggregate subnational level, the horizontal gap takes into account that there can be differences between expenditures and own-revenues for particular subnational governments (due to different abilities to raise revenues and/or differences in their respective needs and costs of providing public services) even when there is no vertical gap. Equalization transfers are the main instrument to fill horizontal gaps.

Abstracting from the larger question of what a desirable or 'optimal' vertical gap would be in a particular country and which spending and revenue responsibilities to decentralize, the concept of horizontal gaps is pertinent in the discussion of natural resource-based transfers from the central government to subnational governments. Accepting that reducing horizontal gaps is a desirable policy goal (so that subnational governments can provide comparable levels of public services at comparable tax rates), strengthens the case for either distributing resource rents more broadly than only to producer regions, or setting up offsetting equalization transfers.

Given this, when the opportunity exists for substantive reforms to decentralization frameworks, those reforms should aim to minimize horizontal inequities (for example, by taking greater account of spending needs), avoid boom-bust revenue cycles at the local level, and, crucially, clarify the goals of the revenue-sharing agreement. To help avoid boom-bust cycles leading to large spending shocks, further use could be made of precautionary stabilization funds with clear rules and governance arrangements, such as in Chile, Colombia, and Norway. To reduce horizontal inequities, the reform of royalty-sharing arrangements in Colombia in 2012 is a good example of what can be done.[5] Having said that, highlighting the difficulty in striking the right balance, the 2019 reform in Colombia was based on criticism that the 2012 setup had removed incentives for municipalities to host natural resource extraction.

[5]Colombia's royalty sharing arrangements are not fully integrated into the annual budget. A unified budget would be a preferable option for most countries.

Achieving consensus on larger reforms of revenue-sharing arrangements is difficult. Transfer arrangements should also be made as transparent as possible to facilitate planning and oversight. Such measures will increase ownership and accountability and reduce revenue volatility. Nonresource transfers can potentially be used to offset some of the horizontal inequities by using measurable criteria of local needs in some of the allocation formulas (for example, the equalization scheme in Canada). As noted in ECLAC (2019), within country regional inequality is particularly high in Latin America, with the ratio of GDP per capita in the richest regions often more than six times higher than in the poorest regions (relative to 3:1 in most developed countries), strengthening the case for including poverty or related measures in transfer formulas.

Other steps can also play a crucial role, including building capacity at the subnational level and encouraging local governments to build their own-revenue bases to reduce reliance on transfers. Property taxes can play an important role in that respect. Currently property tax revenues across the region are still modest at 0.3 percent of GDP on average, due to factors such as weak capacity of subnational governments, lack of updated cadastral values and property registers with weak coverage (ECLAC, 2019). Strengthening property taxation to increase own-revenues of local governments would be an important step, also due to the progressive nature of such as tax given that real estate holdings tend to be concentrated in wealthier households.

Structural Polices

As the analysis has shown, employment (and labor income gains more generally) were key for poverty reduction during the boom. Given this, *labor market reform* and deploying *policies aimed at retooling workers* should help smooth the necessary adjustment to the rebalancing of demand caused by lower commodity prices and support further poverty reduction in the medium term. And such adjustment and the accompanying reallocation will be even more important in the aftermath of the COVID-19 shock. While labor market institutions are multidimensional and not easily described by any set of indicators, it appears that especially South America does have noticeable rigidities in some key labor market dimensions (David, Lambert and Toscani 2019; 2019 *Regional Economic Outlook: Western Hemisphere*). Redundancy costs are higher than in advanced economies (AEs) or other EMDEs, permanent contracts are mandatory for permanent tasks in many countries, and dismissal of even one worker often requires third-party approval (Figure 58).

And certain dimensions of stricter employment protection legislation increase informality, most notably higher redundancy costs and cumbersome dismissal regulations appear to be associated with higher informality. In Latin America,

Figure 58. Labor Market Rigidity across Country Groups

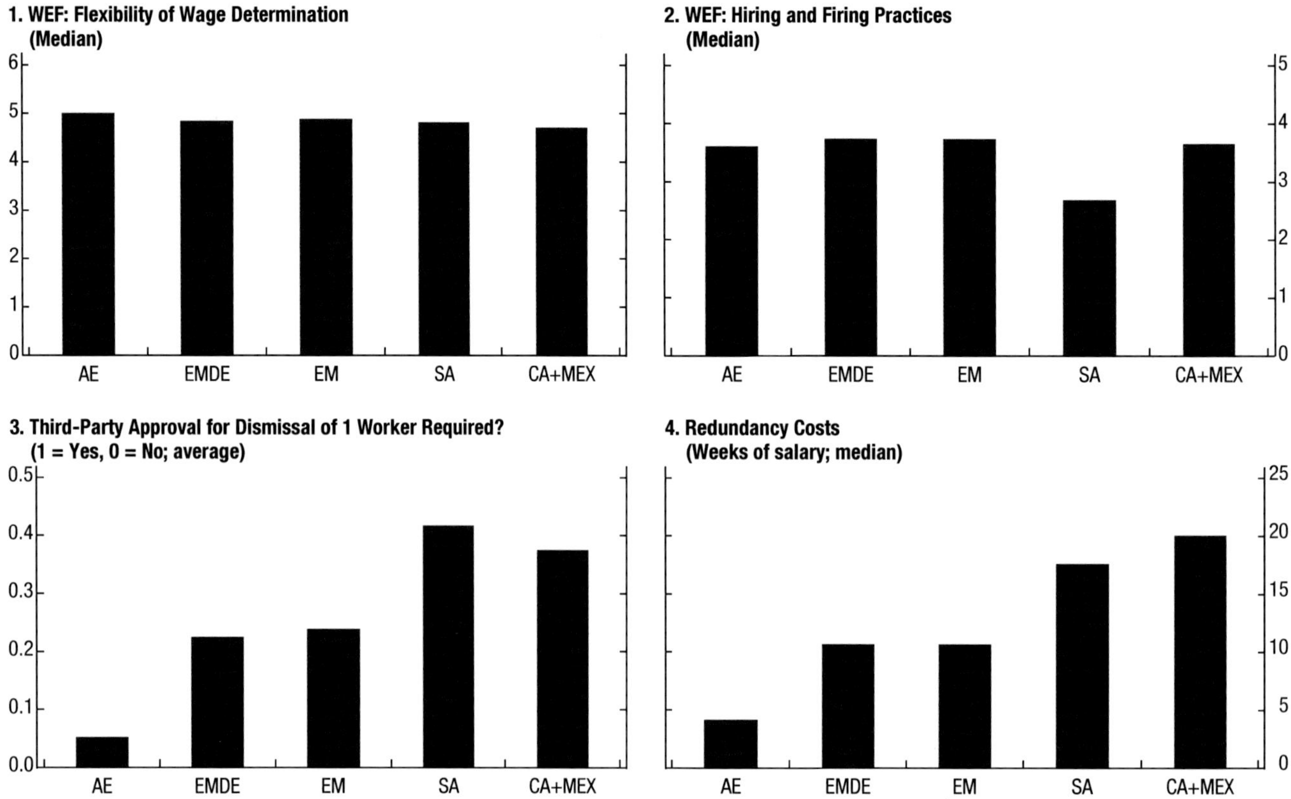

Sources: Organisation for Economic Co-operation and Development, Employment Protection; World Bank, Doing Business Indicators; World Economic Forum (WEF), Global Competitiveness Index; and International Labour Organization, EPLex.
Note: All values are for 2017, except for EPLex data (values are for 2010) and OECD EPL (values are for 2013). AE = advanced economies; EMDE = emerging market and developing economies; SA = South America; CA+MEX = Central America + Mexico.

for instance, Peru and Mexico are two of the countries which have the highest informality relative to their level of development, and also have among the strictest employment protection measures in the dimensions which we show matter for informality (requiring third-party approval for dismissal of even one worker, for example).

Informality, in turn, plays a crucial role in the dynamics of labor markets in Latin America. The response of informality to GDP cycles is estimated to be stronger than that of unemployment. Moreover, estimates of Okun's law show that the formal/informal adjustment margin reduces the importance of the employment/unemployment margin (2019 *Regional Economic Outlook: Western Hemisphere*).[6]

[6]Recall also the above discussion of pensions—higher labor formality, that is, higher contributive pension coverage, is a crucial component to raise old-age income across the region.

Duval and Loungani (2019) recommend that reducing the expected cost of firing procedures, making them more transparent, predictable, and less administratively burdensome, is likely to be an important way to tackle informality and ultimately further improve the functioning of Latin American labor markets. Duval and Loungani (2019) also highlight the importance of building up unemployment insurance and other benefits at the same time to guarantee adequate protection of workers. The exact impact of these recommendations, however, will depend on the nature of informality in each country and how they interact with country institutions and other costs of doing business.

Given that *better education* was an important structural factor that helped reduce inequality and lift people out of poverty during the boom, pushing for further improvements in the quality of education should remain a priority, although gains from any policy measures will take time and only accrue in the longer term. A particular problem is that the Gini index for the distribution of years of education remains high in many countries in LA, particularly Central America where it can reach as much as 0.51 in Guatemala. A concrete way to see this is to consider the difference in the number of years of schooling of the highest income quintile relative to the lowest income quintile (Figure 59). While Argentina stands out with a relatively small difference in the years of education between high income and low-income households, in most LA countries the gap remains very pronounced. The bottom income quintile on average have only six years of education, while the top quintile completed 12, implying a difference of six years of education (or 100 percent when measured relative to the level in the bottom quintile).

To increase progressivity and make opportunities more equal, improving access to primary and lower-secondary education, especially for girls (given large gender gaps) and in rural areas could play an important role. Moreover, despite relatively high public education spending in some LA countries, international test scores for high school students remain relatively low (Figure 60). This suggests significant scope to increase the efficiency of spending in LA.

Tertiary education also plays an important role. Since much of benefit from tertiary education accrues to graduates in the form of higher earnings and other benefits, there is a strong case that graduates finance some of the costs (IMF 2014a). Income-contingent student loans that only need to be paid off when students start earning would ensure that higher education is free at point of use and reduce disincentives for poorer students. These could be additionally reduced by means-testing tuition fees and scholarships, hence ensuring provision of tertiary education remains as progressive as possible.

Last but certainly not least, the most effective long-term policy in making an economy resilient to the effects of a commodity bust is *economic*

Figure 59. Years of Schooling
(Difference, highest and lowest income group)

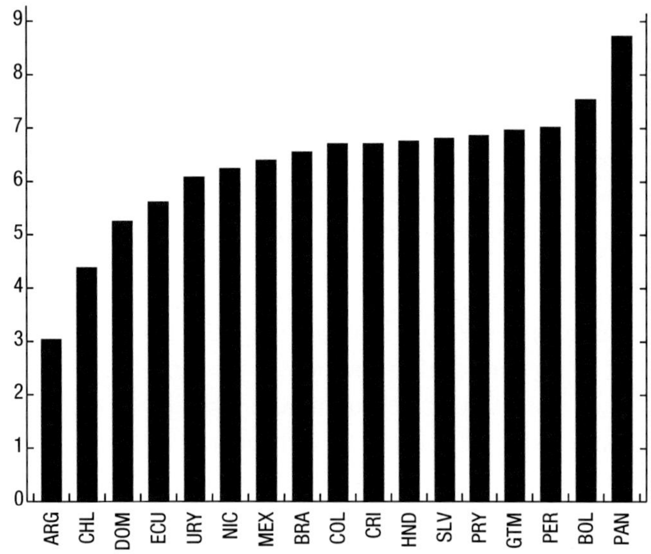

Sources: Socio-Economic Database for Latin America and the Caribbean (CEDLAS and The World Bank); and IMF staff calculations.
Note: Data cover adults aged 25–64. Latest available data for years between 2014 and 2017, depending on the country. Country list uses International Organization for Standardization (ISO) country codes.

Figure 60. Average PISA Scores

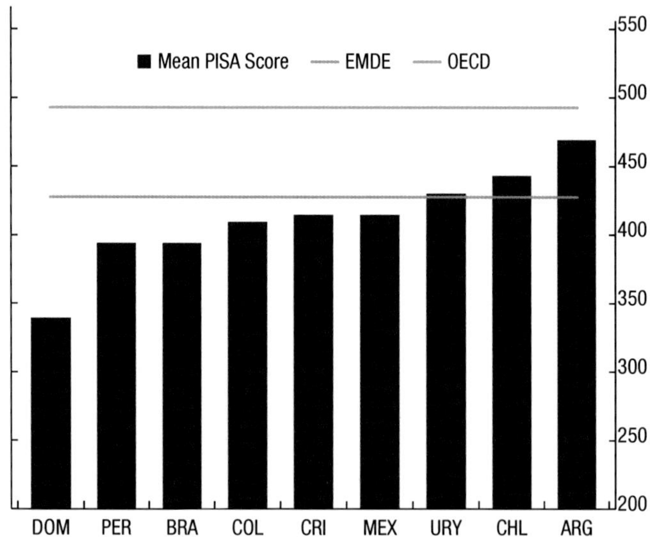

Sources: Organisation for Economic Co-operation and Development (OECD), PISA 2015 Database, Tables I.2.4a, I.2.6, I.2.7, I.4.4a and I.5.4a; and IMF staff calculations.
Note: EMDE (emerging market and developing economies) is calculated as the simple average of available EMDE countries in the dataset excluding LAC. PISA = Programme for International Student Assessment.

diversification. This is even more challenging for commodity producers: while natural resource wealth helps increase living standards, it can also give rise to "Dutch disease" and crimp growth in other tradable sectors, including high-technology manufacturing and services that are often key to escaping the middle-income trap.

As argued in Cherif, Hasanov, and Zhu (2015), perhaps given the structural challenges are so formidable in commodity producers, the "leading hand of the state" can play an important role in a diversification strategy. This could involve an array of policy instruments, including "access to financing and business support services through VC funds, development banks, export promotion agencies, the creation of special economic zones, industry clusters, etc." Studying strategies in countries which have successfully diversified, for example, Korea, Malaysia, and Singapore could be a good starting point. The case of Malaysia is particularly pertinent as it is also a commodity producer.

The case of the agro-export boom in Peru, a traditional exporter of mining products, is also interesting. According to IMF (2020a), the boom would not have been possible without the construction of irrigation districts (which converted desertic areas near the coast into farmland), the existence of several free trade agreements, and the diligent work of the phytosanitary authority (SENASA), which contributed to opening new markets. To achieve further growth of the sector, new investments in irrigation, roads, and ports are needed to extend farmland and reduce transportation and logistics costs.

In terms of the best time to implement diversification policies, to some degree they may be easier to implement in periods of commodity busts as opportunity costs are low and exchange rate depreciations can help nascent exporting sectors. Diversification strategies can start with fostering backwards and forwards links between the commodity sectors and other sectors but then those sectors need to develop their own independent production portfolio to avoid suffering from a commodity bust. Another consideration is that while some diversification policies are easier to implement during bust times, others are more affordable when commodity prices are high and ampler fiscal resource can be exploited. This suggests there are important sequencing tradeoffs to take into account when designing diversification policies.

Of course, the list of policies presented here is not exhaustive and other reforms such as improved governance and rule of law, better access to and quality of health, or expanding financial access by leveraging fintech, can all play important roles in reducing inequality of opportunity, inequality of outcomes and poverty.

Last, it is important to acknowledge the *political economy dimension of reforms*. A recent IMF study (Ciminelli and others 2019) lays out several important considerations in that regard. Reforms should always be carefully designed and prioritized based on good communication and transparency to ensure broad-based support. It is also important that policymakers factor in and address upfront any possible adverse short-term effects of reforms. For example, certain labor market reforms might have adverse effect in the short term, especially when implemented during bad times, while being beneficial in the longer term (IMF 2019b). Fiscal incentives and policies (such as job search assistance, retraining, and stronger social safety nets) to support those who are most affected by reforms may help advance the reform agenda by mitigating potential social and distributional costs.

Concluding Considerations

Since the turn of the century Latin America has enjoyed a period of significant social gains, especially in commodity exporters. But following the end of the commodity boom, the speed of gains slowed and, in some cases, partially reversed. Then the COVID-19 shock hit, likely wiping off years of social progress. Going forward Latin America, and especially South America, faces critical challenges in first recovering from the COVID-19 shock and then achieving further reductions in poverty and inequality.

It is interesting to note that countries such as Argentina, Bolivia, and Ecuador whose governments had a particular focus of reducing inequality—and have been labeled "populists" by some (for example, Edwards 2019)—did indeed record the largest social gains during the commodity boom period. At the same time, they were also the countries with some of the most favorable terms of trade developments. In the aftermath of the boom, the reversal in commodity terms of trade hit them hard, leading to sharply increased fiscal deficits, the need for fiscal adjustment—especially in the case of Argentina and Ecuador—and some reversal in earlier poverty reduction. According to Vuletin and Vegh (2017), fiscal policy was procyclical in Argentina, Brazil, Bolivia, and Ecuador during 2007–16 while it was counter-cyclical in Chile, Colombia, Paraguay, and Peru. An open question is whether there might be complex trade-offs between a focus on achieving social gains quickly and compromising fiscal sustainability (and thus social gains) in the longer term. It is too early to be able to answer this definitely in the context of the recent Latin American experience. But what is clear is that to achieve lasting social gains, governments have to strive to meet both objectives—redistribution and sustainability—at the same time.

Despite previous gains, as a region Latin America still faces acute challenges, especially when it comes to inequality, which is among the highest in the world. Against a background of increased social unrest in 2019 in many commodity exporters across South America, tackling these issues is especially important. And with the COVID-19 shock further exacerbating inequities and social tensions while also reducing fiscal space as governments step in to contain the pandemic and support their economies, the challenge is more formidable than ever. Some positive news comes from commodity terms of trade having recently reached their highest levels since 2011 for Latin American commodity exporters. This, however, will not be sufficient to durably reduce poverty and inequality. The volatile nature of commodity prices means that today's gains can be tomorrow's losses, as we saw when commodity boom turned to commodity bust after 2014.

Although there is no silver bullet, crisis can also be an opportunity for reform and Latin America should use the current one to move ahead and address many of the structural issues that are key to meeting one of the most important challenges in Latin America and the world today.

Box 6. Details of Natural Resource Revenue-Sharing in Latin America and Elsewhere

Natural resource revenues are largely centralized in Chile, Ecuador, Mexico, Norway, Trinidad and Tobago, and Venezuela, with either very limited or no redistribution to subnational producers. In the three case study countries of Chapter 3 and Colombia, significant amounts go to subnational governments (see Viale 2015 for an overview). In Canada, provinces manage nonrenewable natural resources.

Bolivia: Out of the total 18 percent hydrocarbon royalty, 11 percent goes to producing departments, 6 percent stays with the central government, and 1 percent goes to the lightly populated departments of Pando and Beni. The 32 percent hydrocarbon tax (Impuesto directo a los hidrocarburos – IDH) is allocated in a more complicated way, going to both producing and nonproducing departments as well as municipalities, with 20 percentage points remaining with the central government. Mining royalties are distributed only to producing departments and municipalities, with an 85–15 split between the two. For more details, see IDB (2015).

Brazil: Sixty percent of mineral royalties are distributed directly to the producing municipality (prior to a recent reform this share was 65 percent), while the remainder goes to producing states (15 percent), the federal government (10 percent) and non-producing municipalities which have some connection to minerals (for example, a train line transporting minerals passes through, 15 percent). For oil and gas, the allocation formula is much more complicated, but since the 1997 royalties law, substantial amounts of oil and gas revenues have been distributed to municipalities that either host an onshore oil and gas field or face on offshore oil and gas field. In some cases, royalties can account for over 50 percent of a municipality's revenues.

Canada: In addition to being subject to the federal and provincial corporate income tax, natural resource income is subject to mining taxes, royalties, and land taxes at the provincial level. There is also a fiscal stabilization program that enables the federal government to provide financial assistance to any province faced with a year-over-year decline in nonresource revenues greater than 5 percent and caused by an economic downturn. Finally, Canada has an equalization program to reduce fiscal disparities between provinces. The equalization transfers are unconditional and determined by measuring provinces' ability to raise revenues.

Colombia: Prior to the 2012 reform, roughly 80 percent of royalties went directly to producer departments and municipalities, which only had 17 percent of the population. Following the 2012 reform, this was reduced to roughly 10 percent, with the remainder of the resources assigned to a number of central funds with specific goals.

This box replicates information that was published and up to date at the time of the April 2018 *Regional Economic Outlook: Western Hemisphere.*

Box 6. Details of Natural Resource Revenue-Sharing in Latin America and Elsewhere *(continued)*

About 30 percent is saved in a stabilization fund, 10 percent goes to a science and innovation fund, 10 percent to a regional pension fund, and the remainder is allocated to subnational investment projects with a relatively complex distribution formula based on poverty levels and other factors. As a result, 1,089 municipalities received a share of commodity royalties in 2012 compared to 522 in 2011. A 2019 reform increased the share going to producer regions to 25 percent while also increasing the share being distributed to the poorest municipalities and strengthening the investment focus of royalty use.

Norway: Government revenues from petroleum activities are transferred to the Government Pension Fund Global. Under the fiscal rule, petroleum revenues are phased into the economy gradually. Specifically, over time government spending must not use any of the fund's 'capital, only its expected real return, which is currently estimated at 3 percent. The fiscal rule also provides for petroleum revenue spending to be increased during economic downturns and decreased in during economic upturns.

Peru: Overall, about 60 percent of fiscal revenues from the mining sector go to subnational governments, mainly consisting of mining sector corporate income taxes (canon minero) and mining royalties. There are various canons and they are only transferred to the department where production of the natural resource takes place. Resources are then further distributed within producing departments, resulting in producing provinces and municipalities receiving a large share of the pie. See Santos and Werner (2015, Chapter 10) for more details.

Appendix 1. Details of the Model from Chapter 4

The model is a dynamic general equilibrium model of a small open economy with multiple sectors. There are a large number of households that are heterogeneous, both within and across sectors. Urban and rural households differ with respect to their occupations as well as to their access to financial intermediaries. Within-sector heterogeneity is due to household specific shocks to productivity.

Economic Sectors

There are four types of occupations in the economy, three urban and one rural:

- Agricultural workers (rural)
- Entrepreneurs (urban)
- Public-sector workers (urban)
- Private-sector workers (urban)

Households are confined to their sectors and cannot easily switch occupations.

Production

Agricultural workers use their own labor to produce either maize, or other agricultural goods. Agricultural workers differ in their land holdings (some are small farmers and others own large plots) and employ land and labor and fertilizer to produce.

Table 12. Production Structure

Good	Producer	Input	Use
Agricultural goods	Agricultural workers	Land, labor, fertilizer	Consumption, and input production of agricultural exports
Manufacturing	Entrepreneurs	Private sector labor, capital, and energy	Consumption, investment, Exports
Services	Private / public sector workers Entrepreneurs	Informal technology Private sector labor, capital and energy	Consumption, investment
Energy (i.e., oil, natural gas)	Entrepreneurs	Capital	Consumption, Exports
Agricultural export	Entrepreneurs	Domestic food product, private sector labor	Export

Source: IMF staff.

Public-sector workers work for the government which does not produce marketable goods. Private-sector workers provide their labor to the entrepreneurs. Additionally, both private- and public-sector workers devote some of their time to producing services.[1]

The entrepreneurs produce manufacturing and services using capital, labor, and energy.[2] Manufacturing goods can then either be sold to consumers or converted into capital, because they are tradable goods their price is determined in international markets. Services are produced only for the domestic market. Each entrepreneurial household owns its own capital stock which cannot be converted back into manufacturing goods. Capital depreciates over time, so that new investments are necessary to maintain the capital stock.

Entrepreneurs also produce energy goods using a capital-intensive technology. Energy (gas in the case of Republic of Congo) is also a tradable good, and therefore its price is determined in international markets. However, the domestic price of this input is administered by the government.

Besides the domestically produced food item, the industrial goods (services and manufacturing) and energy, there is also an agricultural export product. The production of this good (for example agricultural commodities) takes place in firms owned by entrepreneurs. It uses the food item as input which is then refined and packaged using labor.

Preferences and Household Decisions

Households live forever and are forward looking. In every period, they decide how much of their disposable income to consume and how much to save. Households face uncertainty regarding their future income and are risk averse: they want to avoid large fluctuations of their consumption over time. Having access to a financial intermediary allows them to accumulate a buffer of financial wealth as insurance against future drops in income. Households

[1]This assumption is made to capture large informal sectors in Bolivia and Paraguay.

[2]Hence services are produced both within the entrepreneurs' firms and informally by workers at home.

facing more severe shocks can borrow to smooth consumption if they have access to finance.[3]

Only private- and public-sector workers and a given fraction of agricultural workers have access to finance. The remaining farmers can neither save nor borrow.

Households also decide how to allocate their consumption expenditure over two food items (domestic agricultural goods and imported food) and the non-food goods (manufacturing, services and energy).

Workers also make a decision on how much of their time to devote to the formal labor market and how much to work in the informal sector.

Financial Intermediation and Financial Sector Policies

Financial intermediaries have two distinct roles in the economy:

- They convert manufacturing and services goods into capital.
- They allow households to save and borrow.

Fiscal Policy Parameters

The government in the model has access to a rich set of gas and non-gas taxes and transfers to pay the public sector workers, to finance subsidies, and to provide insurance to vulnerable households. Additionally, the government invests in infrastructure. These policies are captured by a set of exogenous policy parameters:

- A tax on entrepreneurs' capital income
- A tax on private- and public-sector workers' wage earnings
- Royalties from energy sector
- Sector-specific and means-tested transfers and subsidies

Idiosyncratic Shocks

Each non-entrepreneurial household's productivity is subject to random changes over time, but these changes in productivity are different across households. At each point in time, some households are lucky while others

[3]The model thereby highlights the role of financial inclusion not just as a measure of mobilizing resources for investment but also as an insurance mechanism that reduces consumption inequality.

are unlucky. There is no aggregate uncertainty and, given the large number of households, a law of large numbers applies, so that the distribution of shocks across households within each sector remains constant. That is, the number of unlucky households is always the same.

Equilibrium and Steady State

At each point in time, prices, wages, and interest rates are set to ensure that the markets for credit, labor and the goods produced only for domestic consumption clear. Moreover, given these prices (both in the present and future) and government policies, all household decisions are made to maximize the present value of lifetime utility. The prices of energy, agricultural exports and manufacturing goods are exogenously given.

The economy is in a steady state. Aggregate variables and prices are constant over time, as is the distribution of wealth, income, and consumption across households. The income, wealth, and consumption of individual households however changes over time with the realization of their idiosyncratic shocks.

References

Acemoglu, D., S. Johnson, and J. Robinson. 2001. "The Colonial Origins of Comparative Development: An Empirical Investigation." *The American Economic Review* 91(5): 1369–401.

Acemoglu, D., S. Johnson, and J. Robinson. 2002. "Reversal of Fortune: Geography and Institutions in the Making of the Modern World Income Distribution." *The Quarterly Journal of Economics* 117(4): 1231–294.

Aiyagari, S. R. 1994. "Uninsured Idiosyncratic Risk and Aggregate Saving." *The Quarterly Journal of Economics* 109(3): 659–84.

Alberola, E., and G. Benigno. 2017. "Revisiting the Commodity Curse: A Financial Perspective." *Journal of International Economics* 108 (1): 87–106.

Allcott, H., and D. Keniston. 2018. "Dutch Disease or Agglomeration? The Local Economic Effects of Natural Resource Booms in Modern America." *Review of Economic Studies* 85(2): 695–731.

Altamirano, A., S. Berstein, M. Bosch, M. Garcia Huitrón, and M. L. Oliveri, 2018. "Present and Future of Pensions in Latin America and the Caribbean." Inter-American Development Bank, Washington, DC.

Alvarez, R., A. Garcia, and S. Ilabaca. 2017. "Commodity Prices Shocks and Poverty Reducation in Chile." Universidad de Chile Working Paper Series SDT 449, Santiago.

Aragon, F. M., and J. P. Rud. 2013. "Natural Resources and Local Communities: Evidence from a Peruvian Gold Mine." *American Economic Journal: Economic Policy* 5(2): 1–25.

Arellano, M., and S. Bond. 1991. "Some Tests of Specification for Panel Data: Monte Carlo Evidence and an Application to Employment Equations." *Review of Economic Studies* 58(2): 277–97.

Arellano-Yanguas, J. 2011. "Aggravating the Resource Curse: Decentralisation, Mining and Conflict in Peru." *The Journal of Development Studies* 47(4): 617–38.

Arezki, R. F. van der Ploeg, and F. Toscani. 2019. "The Shifting Natural Wealth of Nations: The Role of Market Orientation." *Journal of Development Economics* 138: 228–45.

Azevedo, J. P., G. Inchauste, and V. Sanfelice. 2013. "Decomposing the Recent Inequality Decline in Latin America." Policy Research Working Paper 6315, World Bank, Washington, DC.

Azevedo, J. P., J. Saavedra, and H. Winkler. 2012. "When Job Earnings Are Behind Poverty Reduction." Other Operational Studies Paper 97, World Bank, Washington, DC.

Azevedo, J. P., G. Inchauste, S. Olivieri, J. Saavedra, and V. Sanfelice. 2013. "Is Labor Income Responsible for Poverty Reduction? A Decomposition Approach." Policy Research Working Paper 6414, World Bank, Washington, DC.

Balakrishnan, R., S. Lizarazo, A. Peralta-Alva and M. Mendes Tavares. 2017. "Commodity Boom and Bust and Income Inequality." Unpublished, International Monetary Fund, Washington, DC.

Barros, R., M. Carvalho, S. Franco, and R. Mendonça. 2006. "An Analysis of the Main Causes of the Recent Fall in Brazilian Income Inequality." 1203, Discussion Papers, Institute of Applied Economic Research (IPEA), Brasilia.

Barros, Ricardo, Francisco H. G. Ferreira, Jose Molinas, and Jaime Saavedra. 2009. *Measuring Inequality of Opportunity in Latin America and the Caribbean.* Washington, DC: World Bank.

Barros, R., M. De Carvalho, S. Franco, and R. Mendonça. 2010. "Markets, the State and the Dynamics of Inequality in Brazil." In *Declining Inequality in Latin America: A Decade of Progress?* Edited by L. F. Lopez-Calva and N. Lustig. Washington, DC: Brookings Institution and UNDP.

Barros, R., F. H. G. Ferreira, J.R.M. Vega, and J.S. Chanduvi. 2012. *Measuring Inequality of Opportunities in Latin America and the Caribbean.* Latin American Development Forum, Washington, DC: World Bank.

Benavidies, P., and R. Valdés. 2018. "Pensiones en Chile: antecedentes y contornos para una reforma urgente." Centro de Politicas Publicas UC, Número 107.

Benguria, F., F. Saffie, and S. Urzua. 2018. "The Transmission of Commodity Price Super-Cycles." NBER Working Paper 24560, National Bureau of Economic Research, Cambridge, MA.

Boadway, R., and L. Eyraud. 2018. "Designing Sound Fiscal Relations Across Government Levels in Decentralized Countries." IMF Working Paper 18/271, International Monetary Fund, Washington, DC.

Bottan, N. L., D. A. Vera-Cossio and B. Hoffmann, 2020. "The Unequal Impact of the Coronavirus Pandemic: Evidence from Seventeen Developing Countries", Discussion Paper IDB-DP-785. Inter-American Development Bank. Washington, DC.

Campos-Vazquez, R. M., G. Esquivel, and N. Lustig. 2012. "The Rise and Fall of Income Inequality in Mexico, 1989–2010." United Nations University Working Paper 10/2012, New York.

Caselli. F., and G. Michaels. 2013. "Do Oil Windfalls Improve Living Standards? Evidence from Brazil." *American Economic Journal: Applied Economics* 51: 208–38.

Cavalcanti, T., D. Da Mata, and F. Toscani. 2019. "Winning the Oil Lottery: The Impact of Natural Resource Discoveries on Growth." *Journal of Economic Growth* 24 (1): 79–115.

Ciminelli, G., D. Furceri, J. Ge, J. D. Ostry, and C. Papageorgiou. 2019. "The Political Costs of Reforms: Fear or Reality?" IMF Staff Discussion Note, International Monetary Fund, Washington, DC.

Cherif, R., F. Hasanov, and M. Zhu. 2015. *Breaking the Oil Spell.* Washington, DC: International Monetary Fund.

Cornia, G., and B. Martorano. 2013. "Development Policies and Income Inequality in Selected Developing Regions, 1980–2010." Economic Working Paper. University of Florence, Department of Economics and Business Sciences, Florence.

Cornia, G.A. 2014. *Falling Inequality in Latin America: Policy Changes and Lessons.* Oxford: Oxford University Press.

Cruces, G., and L. Gasparini. 2011. "Inequality in Education: Evidence for Latin America." WIDER Working Paper Series 093, World Institute for Development Economic Research (UNU-WIDER), Helsinki.

Cust, J., and S. Poelhekke. 2015. "The Local Economic Impacts of Natural Resource Extraction." *Annual Review of Resource Economics* 7 (5): 215–68.

David, A., F. Lambert, and F. Toscani. 2019. "More Work to Do? Taking Stock of Latin American Labor Markets." IMF Working Paper 19/55, International Monetary Fund, Washington, DC.

De la Torre, Augusto, J. Messina, and S. Pienknagura. 2012. "The Labor Market Story Behind Latin America's Transformation." LAC Semiannual Report (October). World Bank, Washington, DC.

De la Torre, Augusto, A. Ize, G. R. Beylis, and D. Lederman. 2015. *Jobs, Wages, and the Latin American Slowdown*. Washington, DC: World Bank Group.

Duval, R., and P. Loungani. 2018. "Designing Labor Market Institutions in Emerging and Frontier Economies: Evidence and IMF Advice." IMF Staff Discussion Note 19/04, International Monetary Fund, Washington, DC.

Economic Commission for Latin America and the Caribbean (ECLAC). 2017. "Social Panorama of Latin America 2017." Santiago.

Economic Commission for Latin America and the Caribbean (ECLAC). 2018. "Social Panorama of Latin America 2018." Santiago.

Economic Commission for Latin America and the Caribbean (ECLAC). 2019. "Fiscal Panorama of Latin America and the Caribbean 2019." Santiago.

Edwards, S. 2019. "On Latin American Populism, and Its Echoes around the World." *Journal of Economic Perspectives* 33 (4): 76–99.

Engerman, S., and K. Sokoloff. 1997. "Factor Endowments: Institutions, and Differential Paths of Growth Among New World Economies: A View from Economic Historians of the United States." In *How Latin America Fell Behind*, edited by Stephen Haber. Palo Alto, CA: Stanford University Press.

Engerman, S., and K. Sokoloff. 2000. "Institutions, Factor Endowments, and Paths of Development in the New World." *Journal of Economic Perspectives* 14 (3): 217–32.

Engerman, S., and K. Sokoloff. 2002. "Factor Endowments, Inequality, and Paths of Development Among New World Economics." NBER Working Pape 9259, National Bureau of Economic Research, Cambridge, MA.

Feres, J. C., and X. Mancero. 2001. "El Metodo de las necesidades basicas insatisfechas (NBI) y sus aplicaciones en America Latina." Economic Commission for Latin America and the Caribbean, Santiago.

Ferreira, F. H. G., and J. Gignoux. 2011. "The Measurement of Inequality of Opportunity: Theory and Application for Latin America" *Review of Income and Wealth* 57 (4): 622–57.

Ferreira, F. H. G., and V. Peragine. 2016. "Individual Responsibility and Equality of Opportunity."In *The Oxford Handbook of Well-Being and Public Policy*, edited by M. D. Adler and M. Fleurbaey. Oxford: Oxford University Press.

Figliuoli, L. V. Flamini, R. Mowatt, J. Puig, F. Lambert, B. Lissovolik, M. Galdamez, M. Li, A. Klemm, M. Soto, S. Thomas, C. Freudenberg, and A. Orthofer. "Growing Pains Is Latin America Prepared for Population

Aging?" Departmental Paper Series, Western Hemisphere Department, International Monetary Fund. Washington, DC.

Freudenberg, C., and F. Toscani, 2019. "Informality and the Challenge of Pension Adequacy: Outlook and Reform Options for Peru." IMF Working Paper 19/149, International Monetary Fund, Washington, DC.

Gasparini, L., and N. Lustig. 2011. "The Rise and Fall of Income Inequality in Latin America." ECINEQ Working Paper Series 2011–213, Society for the Study of Economic Inequality, Palma de Mallorca.

Goes, C., and I. Karpowicz. 2017. "Inequality in Brazil: A Regional Perspective." IMF Working Paper 17/225, International Monetary Fund, Washington, DC.

Gollin, D., S. Parente, and R. Rogerson. 2006. "The Food Problem and the Evolution of International Income Levels." *Journal of Monetary Economics* 54: 1230–55.

Greenwood, J., Z. Hercowitz, and P. Krusell. 1997. "Long-Run Implication of Investment-Specific Technological Change." *American Economic Review* 87: 342–62.

Gruss, B. 2014. "After the Boom – Commodity Prices and Economic Growth in Latin America and the Caribbean." IMF Working Paper 14/154, International Monetary Fund, Washington DC.

Gruss, B., and S. Kebhaj, 2019. "Commodity Terms of Trade: A New Database." IMF Working Paper 19/21, International Monetary Fund, Washington DC.

Hanni, M., R. Martner, and A. Podesta. 2015. "The Redistributive Potential of Taxation in Latin America." *CEPAL Review* 116: 8–26.

Harding, T., and A.J. Venables. 2016. "The Implications of Natural Resource Exports for Nonresource Trade." *IMF Economic Review* 64 (2): 268–302

Herrendorf, B., C. Herrington, and A. Valentinyi. 2015. "Sectoral Technology and Structural Transformation." *American Economic Journal: Macroeconomics* 7 (4): 104–33.

Inter-American Development Bank (IDB). 2015. *Decentralizing Revenue in Latin America: Why and How.* Washington, DC.

International Monetary Fund (IMF). 2009. "Macro Policy Lessons for a Sound Design of Fiscal Decentralization." IMF Fiscal Affairs Department, Washington, DC.

International Monetary Fund (IMF). 2014a. "Fiscal Policy and Income Inequality." IMF Fiscal Affairs Department, Washington, DC.

International Monetary Fund (IMF). 2014b. "Congo: Selected Issues." Washington, DC.

International Monetary Fund (IMF). 2017. "Uruguay: Selected Issues." Washington, DC.

International Monetary Fund (IMF). 2018a. *Regional Economic Outlook: Western Hemisphere*, Chapter 5, April, Washington, DC.

International Monetary Fund (IMF). 2018b. "Colombia – 2018 Article IV Consultation." Washington, DC.

International Monetary Fund (IMF). 2018c. "Mexico – 2018 Article IV Consultation." Washington, DC.

International Monetary Fund (IMF). 2019a. *Regional Economic Outlook: Western Hemisphere,* Washington, DC, October.

International Monetary Fund (IMF). 2019b. *World Economic Outlook*, Washington, DC, October.

International Monetary Fund (IMF). 2020a. "Peru – 2019 Article IV Consultation." Washington D.C.

International Monetary Fund (IMF). 2020b. *Regional Economic Outlook: Western Hemisphere*, October, Washington, DC.

Lambert, F., and H. Park. 2019. "Income Inequality and Government Transfers in Mexico." IMF Working Paper 19/148, International Monetary Fund, Washington, DC.

Loayza, N., and J. Rigolini. 2014. "The Local Impact of Mining on Poverty and Inequality: Evidence from the Commodity Boom in Peru." Peruvian Economic Association Working Paper 33, Lima.

López-Calva, L., and N. Lustig. 2010. *Declining Inequality in Latin America: A Decade of Progress?* Washington, DC: Brookings Institution Press.

Lustig, N. 2018. *Commitment to Equity Handbook*. Washington, DC: Brookings Institution.

Lustig, N. 2012. "Taxes, Transfers, and Income Redistribution in Latin America." *Inequality in Focus* 1 (2).

Lustig, N., L. F. Lopez-Calva, and E. Ortiz-Juarez. 2012. "Declining Inequality in Latin America in the 2000s: The Cases of Argentina, Brazil, and Mexico." Working Paper 266, Society for the Study of Economic Inequality, Palma de Mallorca.

Lustig, N., L. F. Lopez-Calva, and E. Ortiz-Juarez. 2013. "Deconstructing the Decline in Inequality in Latin America." Policy Research Working Paper 6552, World Bank, Washington, DC.

Lustig, N., V. Martinez Pabon, F. Sanz and S.D. Younger, 2020, "The Impact of COVID-19 Lockdowns and Expanded Social Assistance on Inequality, Poverty and Mobility in Argentina, Brazil, Colombia and Mexico," CEQ Institute, Working Paper 92.

Messina, J., and J. Silva. 2018. *Wage Inequality in Latin America: Understanding the Past to Prepare for the Future*. Washington, DC: World Bank.

Michaels, G. 2011. "The Long-term Consequences of Resource-based Specialization." *Economic Journal* 121 (551): 31–57.

Nishiyama, S., and K. Smetters. 2005. "Consumption Taxes and Economic Efficiency with Idiosyncratic Wage Shocks." *Journal of Political Economy* 113 (5): 1088–115.

Nishiyama, S., and K. Smetters. 2007. "Does Social Security Privatization Produce Efficiency Gains?" *The Quarterly Journal of Economics* 122 (4): 1677–719.

Organisation for Economic Co-operation and Development (OECD). 2018. *Revenue Statistics in Latin America and the Caribbean 2018.* Paris: OECD Publishing.

Pellandra, A. 2015. "The Commodity Price Boom and Regional Workers in Chile: A Natural Resources Blessing?" Unpublished.

Perry G., and M. Olivera. 2009. "El Impacto del Petróleo y la Minería en el Desarrollo Regional y Local en Colombia." CAF Working Paper 2009/06, CAF Development Bank of Latin America, Caracas.

Rawls, J. 1971. *A Theory of Justice.* Cambridge, MA: Harvard University Press.

Restuccia, D., T. Dennis, X. and Zhu. 2008. "Agriculture and Aggregate Productivity: A Quantitative Cross-Country Analysis." *Journal of Monetary Economics* 55: 234–50.

Romer, J., and A. Trannoy. 2015. "Equality of Opportunity." In *Handbook of Income Distribution*, edited by A. Atkinson and F. Bourguignon. Amsterdam: Elsevier.

Santos, A., and A. Werner, eds. 2015. *Peru: Staying the Course of Economic Success.* Washington, DC: International Monetary Fund.

Sastre, M., and A. Trannoy. 2002, "Shapley Inequality Decomposition by Factor Components: Some Methodological Issues." *Journal of Economics* 9 (1): 51–89.

Solt, F. 2016. "The Standardized World Income Inequality Database." *Social Science Quarterly* 97 (5): 1267–81.

Toscani, F. 2017. "The Impact of Natural Resource Discoveries in Latin America and the Caribbean: A Closer Look at the Case of Bolivia." IMF Working Paper 17/27, International Monetary Fund, Washington, DC.

Tsounta, E., and A. I. Osueke. 2014. "What is Behind Latin America's Declining Income Inequality." IMF Working Paper 14/124, International Monetary Fund, Washington DC.

van der Ploeg, F. 2011. "Natural Resources: Curse or Blessing?" *Journal of Economic Literature* 49 (2): 366–420.

Vargas, J. P. M., and S. Garriga. 2015. "Explaining Inequality and Poverty Reduction in Bolivia." IMF Working Paper 15/265, International Monetary Fund, Washington DC.

Viale, C. 2015. "Distribution of Extractive Industries Income to Subnational Governments in Latin America: Comparative and Trend Analysis." Pontificial Catholic University of Peru, Lima.

Vuletin, G., and C. Vegh. 2017. "Has Latin America Learned to Use Fiscal Policy to Stabilize the Business Cycle?" Brookings Institution, Washington, DC.

World Bank. 2008. *Closing the Coverage Gap: The Role of Social Pensions and Other Retirement Income Transfers*. Washington, DC.

Yamada, G., J. F. Castro, and J. L. Baciagalupo. 2012. "Desigualdad menatria en un contexto de rápido crecimiento económico: El caso reciente del Peru." Revista Estudios Economicos 24: 65–77. Banco Central de Reserva del Peru.